I0580851

Tofu Ink Arts Press

Volume 7

Dedicated to

Hubby, Geo Bowers and the Garlic Poetry Long Beach Loves

"To consecrate the union between elsewhere and possibility, the poet demanded of himself permanent abstinence from something impossible."

- Poetics of Relation, Edouard Glissant

Contents

Natanjah Driscoll Harvey

If I could
Start again, and bellow
All my incandescence
Over a breath that sends
My intention for green things
Over to you where you
Catch wind and say, "hello."

Abol Bahadori

Stretch

Stephen Brown

Boyfriend Materials I

Boyfriends like Bobby sometimes only communicate through vibrations. This one lives on my desk, speaks to me, and other men, through these taps, always at a frequency easy to ignore, his fine-tipped fingers drumming repeatedly on the glass wall of his enclosure, the screen of his phone.

Click, clickclick, I answer back with that clicky part of my pen, watch all his arms and all his legs curl inward, a weak man so shocked by the suddenness of my acknowledgement that he forgets to decipher its meaning.

He need only climb out, and crawl toward me.

Sona Verdi

Crossing

Ali Telmesani

The Isthmus

Wayfarers ask me constantly concerning the in-between.
What then should I say to them? To know is not to know?
I am no keeper of gates, nor a boudoir-guarding eunuch
refusing unsuitables entry to a garden of many waters.
Out of desperation they refuse none other than themselves,
thinking they might slip through the veil actively
when passive receptivity is required to gain entry.

A youth from Bounān in the Northern Yusrāw hinterlands
asked me to perform a miracle, to manufacture a sign,
as if I was a soothsaying discloser of wondrous things.
Within his own sanctum, nearer than the jugular vein,
amid the rapid, fleeting fluctuations of the heart,
the Real through whom creation occurs discloses Herself
at every instant, would that he knew the realities of things.
Had I produced a sparrow, what then would he have requested?
I offered the youth a handful of sand I let slip through my fingers
and the youth from Bounān departed cursing, bemoaning his lot.
Would that he knew: each grain of sand is a storehouse of signs
and names of manifest traces of Her in the corporeal world.

In the cosmos, every *thing* is an isthmus between two things,
sharing the attributes of both--the luminous and the corporeal.
Each sign maps out algorithms of the Divine Womb
that lead to where the two seas meet but never mingle.
Revel in the Knowledge of the wondrous Names of our Creator
that share in the glory of oneness and manyness all at once.
They name the one and only Real, representing the faces
of Her in the multiplicitous domain of Her Creation.
It behoves wayfarers not to forget that wheresoever
they turn, they will find Her face staring right back at them
and nothing other than, for Her face is manyness
itself, sourced from the spring of Her incontrovertible Oneness.

But the Real through whom creation occurs revealed to us
that oneness preceded manyness in the heirarchy of Being--
for without Being, the many categorically could not exist--
much like light preceded colour and mercy preceded wrath.
Know the realities of the One/Many and your place between them.

As the intense angelic light disperses, boundlessly
differentiating the sensory temporal/spatial extension
that is our own existence, the isthmus continues to expand;
and as the microcosm mimics the macrocosm,
we contain those same heirarchic multitudes
that form the ever-expanding terrain between the realms
of supernal dominion and unequivocal non-existence.
Within these borderlines our soul may lean and loaf
as it may between the abodes of mercy and ignorance.

'But what do you see there?' asked another youth from Qaws,
thinking the isthmus is a place of wonders for eyes to behold
when in reality it is the domain of the third eye alone.
How difficult it is to describe the indescribable!
Out of fear of discouraging the youth, I hesitantly revealed
how its canopying sky is a shade that is itself a cypher,
a colour that is a meeting point between light and dark.
Its panoply of lunar bodies not only occupies the empyrean
but hangs and rotates in the ether within touching distance.
The soil is rich and oversaturated with every mineral
and can be fashioned like clay, breathed into and brought to life.
On either shore of the isthmus, the waters are mysterious and dark
with surfaces undisturbed by even the slightest breeze.
Beneath it are untold mysteries of the realities of things
that somehow exist without agitating the still waters.

And what of the entities that populate the isthmus?
What could I have possibly said other than
it is the domain of corporeous entities and spirits
of varied subtlety, of jinn made of smokeless fire,
who occupy the in-between by merit, for they--
much like our selves--are creatures burdened with free will.
There are the spirits of martyrs like Zulaykha of Qurtub,
Taha the Shepherd, Sayf of Erbā and Qamar of Maysawayn,

who sowed what was good, and whose bodies perished,
but whose souls did reap the rewards of the here,
the in-between and the hereafter. There are the spirits
of eternal flame, who exalt unceasingly, whose roles
in the arc of creation are precalculated, who take the form
of celestial and physical bodies that follow Her designs.
Equally are they the souls of the fauna and flora
as they are the souls of Andromeda and Nebula
as they are the souls of the constellation clusters
as they are the souls of careering gaseous orbs
as they are the souls of oceans and their contents
as they are the souls of stars and their stuff,
and the souls of suns, moons and their stuff too.

The beings of Light--the angels and other malā'ika--
they come and go as they please, for their presence
preceded created things in the supreme cosmogeny.
They float freely, they ride in horseless chariots
through the air, across the waters and upon the plain,
moving effortlessly by the will of the unmoved Mover.
Not only are they the couriers of the Divine Reality,
but also the escorts of the prophets who came before,
who were themselves the couriers of the supreme Logos.
They exist eternally, entering and exiting the isthmus freely.
When the Merciful--who is also the Wise and Utmost Real--
disclosed Herself to them, initiating their prophetic mission,
She disclosed Herself in the tongue of their communities,
that the discourse of the Supreme Reality be clear to them.
May their reward from the Merciful be exceedingly bounteous,
for theirs was a sacrifice not one of them wished to make,
for they feared rejection from their own communities,
and when indeed they faced persecution and exile,
they remained steadfast in their prophetic mission,
interceding on behalf of their own communities.

O peace be upon the busy hands and callused soles
of the prophet Nūr of Kunaytara, whose luminescence
filled the hearts and homes of her communities,
empowering those who were made to feel powerless,
emancipating others by her effect on the fragile self,

loosening pride's grip on those willing to debase themselves.
She brought them the Word and brought them a warning,
for she was nothing but a warner of consequential matters,
of the destructive forces that wreak havoc and sow discord
in the earth and in the soil of one's being, which they heeded not.

O peace be upon the busy hands and callused soles
of the prophet Rakkān of Jawāzayn, whose wisdom
increased his community in knowledge of the Alive,
but their hearts did not easily accept the Word as did
their ears, for in their hearts was a sickness and She
increased them in sickness, for they failed to realize
their own wickedness, and when they burned at the stake
the messenger of the Possessor of the Day of Judgment,
the prophet from Jawāzayn gave a final warning,
of the imminence of that Final Hour, which they heeded not.

O peace be upon the busy hands and callused soles
of the prophet Shams of Mādaba, who turned the tombs
of martyrs into shrines and turned the shrines of tyrants
into tombs unfit for the living, for the whisperer in them
brought destruction to whole empires and their peoples.
When the prophet appeared to them with the Truth from the One
Who Takes Account of All Matters, they crucified Shams,
his body inverted, nailed to the cross and left to rot
on the Eastern Road between Jarash and Sufahān--
but the prophet from Mādaba felt not a thing, for his soul
had lifted from its casing and rose up from the world of bodies
through the heavenly stations to the Station of Proximity,
where it would find peace in the Garden of Many Waters,
from which the crucifiers will be refused, for they received
the Truth from the Sublime Witness, to which they paid no heed.

O peace be upon the busy hands and callused soles
of the prophet Asya of Tāshīn, servant of the Sovereign,
whose branded hands bore the mark of servitude
as did her community in the aftermath of conflict,
whose beauty caught the eye of the tyrant of Azrā Kāf
but who served none other than the Hearer of Invocation,
who spoke to Her servant by way of the simurgh and the bee

in the language of archetypes and signs unheard and unseen
disclosing to Asya the mysteries of the supernal dominion
and warning her of the perilous realities of her prophetic mission.
Verily did the prophet of Tāshīn accept her fate,
and verily was she delivered by her beneficent Creator.
And when she returned to face the tyrant of Azrā Kāf
demanding in the name of the Possessor of the Day of Judgment
the emancipation of her downpressed community,
they fed her to the fire. But the Unfailing for her sake
made the fire cool and soothing, and when Asya spoke
from the fire, the tyrant of Azrā Kāf and his retinue
prostrated themselves before her and begged her to intercede
on their behalf, lest they experience the true Fire.
These rightly-guided prophets and many thousands more
access freely the eternal celestial abode of their choosing.
When the youth from Qaws asked me how to meet them
on those shores, I offered him a mustard seed.
He levelled curses, crawled back into himself and departed.
Had he stayed a little longer, I would have divulged
that the path to the isthmus is through the imagination,
for the isthmus is, in reality, the imaginal realm,
through which we may ascend into the world of spirits
and through which the world of spirits may descend to us,
and so it is the watering hole for beings of all stations.
The mechanistic imagination is simply a tool,
where as the imaginal world is both spatial and temporal
but with space and time utterly ungoverned by limitations,
where strictly metaphysical faculties are of any use.

Call the isthmus what you will: the mundus imaginalis,
is nondelimited and contains the totality of heirarchies,
where every impossibility is possible, and where contraries
come together and engage with every other possible thing.
The utterly nondelimited nature of the imaginal realm
makes it the most obvious plane of reality for the Real
to penetrate and disclose Herself. Is She not nearer to us
than the jugular vein? How easy it is for Her to come
to us, and, would that we knew it, how easy it is
to come to Her, whether we are awake or asleep.
When we are truly awake, we are granted unique access

to that aqueous, dreamlike reality between two seas,
free to commune with spirits, prophets and messengers,
free to ponder on the shores of the isthmus in wonderment,
free to interpret the traces of Her Names in all things,
free to produce the fauna of paradise from the clay,
free to forfeit oneself to the peace of ungoverned eons,
free to witness but also touch the lunar and solar bodies,
and to understand their pregnant signs and cyphers.

In the great heirarchy of being, the imaginal mundus is She/
not She--Real, but not Real--neither this nor that, both this
and that, a realm of intrinsic ambiguity where everything
is annihilated except the true faces of things, for the face
of a thing is its true nature, and wheresoever we turn,
whether in the realm of bodies or in the realm of spirits,
wheresoever we look, we testify to what we witness
as we comingle between the realities of She/not She.

"a realm of intrinsic ambiguity where everything is annihilation

Octavio Quintanilla

"Frontextures"

Quiero tocar tu cuerpo con mi noche interna

Aaron Hoge

Lightning & Red Paint

I blast Enlightenment—
a waste of time
doo da doo
Least weasel on rock

Ball lightning explodes
medieval morality,
I shoot off rainbows

"blue fire flashes,"
needing no theology
I walk four borzois

Gas giant sky god
Robotic Spacecraft Welcome
eagles clutch lightning

Aleax on Rings of Saturn,
living double life.
Cleaning teeth w/ Vorpal Blade—
oblivious to it all!

Purple sequined gown
swished off of rack & fluttered
glamour seeks glamour

On Esopus Island,
searching for traces of Crowley
Lightning & red paint

"Bound to the back of a tiger"
longing for delicacy
crashing through a crystal haven

Rebecca won't invoke
I'm afraid of poverty
& all the germs are happy

British & proper
my cousin Lavinia
loves Metallica

green of that happy grass
covered ripely
the green of dreams

Red-tailed hawk
grips white birch branch
black striped bark below

Counting on water
bright yellow attack hose set
red fire engine

Yellow banana
never wanted to be green
self-realization

White-footed mouse drums
there in the red twig dogwood
red stems white berries

Sitting back on psilocybin mushroom
not stoned
but faulty perception has been cured

Playing a game of truth
playing w/ sand
becoming who I am

Sitting in front of a Zen garden
dreaming of the processes of nature
raked sand

When both sides are full of shit,
I'm grateful that I'm not food for the moon.

Desiring a savior
my subconscious mind
produces flying saucers

Disciplined by Walmart Auto Care Center
the wait is long, eternal
but outside the persimmons are a-bloom

Becoming a tiger
by wearing a mask
I become what I display

Tiger mask has its own life
wearing it courts artistic possession
Archetype jumps on back of motorbike

Satan disembedded from Christian demonology,
no longer smiting Job with sore boils.
My friend, the enemy.

Paper lanterns flood the river
wailing the loss of the Titanic
we belong to the Ear

Zeitgeist

21st century America,
the emotional pattern is distorted.
My pleasure in merry-go-rounds is enormous—
Whee!

Nooshin Hakim

Requiem

Eric Wittkopf

Yellow Brick Roads are Always Yellow

There are unseen gifts that
pass between the hands of
boys that only they can give.
Precious to those who ride
to the far island on the dog
boy's amber barge. The
two-headed dog boy wags
the earth with his tail. He
hums a hymn to Valkyries.
Look at him wrong and he
pushes you over the side.
The flash of his gold signet
ring blinds you as he shares
a cigar with himself, tattoos
unfurling a medieval tapestry
of stags and wolves chased
through runic crevasses under
an eyelid that opens if you
lie. A boy might hesitate at
the vortex of earth, sea, fire,
and sky, but not the two-
headed dog boy. He ate his
master for breakfast and he
learned how to pet himself.

In the dining hall on the
island, the gods replaced
your mother with a spotless,
stainless steel cooler that
dispenses milk with a lever,
as much as you want, and
she never complains. You
pour some out between the
megaliths to appease her,

where the winding stairs
dip into the catacombs of
heroes. But for the clash of
dice and dishwashers, the
place is quiet as a library,
the plank tabletops bearing
the history of this place in
carvings of names & dates,
sacrosanct as mausoleums.
Hindsight is always 20/20
to the blind ones. At meals
a prayer rises to the god of
this place in their honor. His
altar is its own dining hall.

He drew you here to see it.
Its sides riot with outlines
of mahogany boys gaming in
relief, but you will not join
them, to your mother's chagrin.
You are a spent cartridge in
an age of compound sorrows.
You shrink on sidelines as
so-called counselors swear
and joke and toss footballs.
The best-looking one hands
you a half-eaten fudgsicle
where you sit half-starved,
knowing at the top of the
tower there are the suits of
armor you will never wear.
His shirt says everyone
should be young at least once,
and maybe, once is enough.
You will sit with friends on
movie night but later you
will lie alone and cry on
your little island, knowing
somewhere there is a boy
waiting for the same ferry
who never appears in credits.

Middle Earth for Losers

In our little orc school Lycée
Gorbag 18 rue M. Morgul we
learn useful things like archery
and how to climb down from
the ceiling on all fours and how
to bite the hands that feed us.
Tolkien wrote our handbook.

Shoving, kicking, punching are
the extracurriculars.   Knocking
our books to the ground. Little
orc threats hang over me like
previews of coming attractions.
On quaint side streets where
older kids are chuffing, I hear
little orc voices crying "FAG!!!"

Across Bd. St.-Germain lies a
grown-up world but I'm sure
I won't make it there alive.
Men in Christian Dior suits
clog every Prancing Pony.
I'm a nerdy hobbit always
craning to see what's around
the corners of Middle Earth.
Hunched against the Nazgul
lurking over us in our beds.

It's the Gandalfs that have all
the power, here. My gym
teacher is a balrog with a
crew cut and a whistle. He
laughs and shakes his head
at me in my oversize shorts.
When I ask for a grade, he
snorts, "You shall not pass."
Vous ne passerez pas, *madame*.

I'm told there's not much
left of medieval Paris but
the tourists love those bits.
They should include us
in their bougie itinerary.

We visited the Conciergerie
on the other side of the Seine,
the pre-Versailles dungeons
of the old palace where they
prepped Marie Antionette
for the guillotine. One more
queen awaiting execution,
dreaming of her d'Artagnan.
Or in this case her Strider.

I'm sure Peter Jackson went
there, as well. It looks like
the Mines of Moria, its
vaulted ceilings and columns
just made for scrabbling orc
hands and feet. For Gollum
watching from the shadows,
shrinking from security cams
of Mordor in the museum.
There's nothing worth stealing.

I looked for your tomb there.
The one that Gandalf finds in
the movie. "Here lies Balin,
son of Fundin, Lord of Moria."
But all I found was a squishy
sock in the men's toilet, now
interred in my school backpack.
The Tomb of the Unknown Gay
Boy. I enjoy standing guard.

You gotta pity Sauron. He's
the loneliest bastard around.
Nobody invites him. Nobody
sends Christmas cards despite
a catchy carol about the rings.
He needs to up his marketing
game. A better return policy.
He is shunned even by actuaries.
Who wants to insure Mt. Doom?

I was glad to escape Paris. It's
nothing like the stories. Think
Galadriel opening a gift shop at
the airport. I only came back to
lay a wreath on Dumas' grave.
Nobody's rescuing me. The
fellowship failed. You were my
Boromir. I was your precious,
ghosting your fingers like honey
leaving a mark that taste hella
good. Now I'm sticking to reality.

On The Madness of Hölderlin by Elsie Russell, 1995 (painting)

Description: Friedrich Hölderlin is struck by Apollo while walking in May, 1802

Brother, that vision of Apollo
shattered you, it seems, and now
there lies between us a gulf of
more than mere centuries

You looked on him and saw
the harbinger of a new age for
mankind in the god of poetry
and sun-drizzled cataclysm

Why not worship him if you
could be one, too? Forgetting,
maybe, that some gods
would rather be left alone

You sought an audience among
Doric columns that protect his
altar from the sun that burns
whatever gets too close to it

Laying your armor down
thinking to cool yourself in
the shade and tipping an oil
lamp onto the parchments

You won't be the last to
entreat Delphi's oracle and
watch the flames consume
what you held most dear

Would you befriend that one
before whom the angel of
death cowered when bearing
his bloodless brother from Troy?

He tamed a centaur's wild heart
before breaking it on the wheel
and slew his beloved Hyacinth
with a look; don't look too close

Only see how near love veers to
madness, how bitterly it strikes
when led astray by fear of losing
what belongs to gods alone

Evan Huey

Untitled

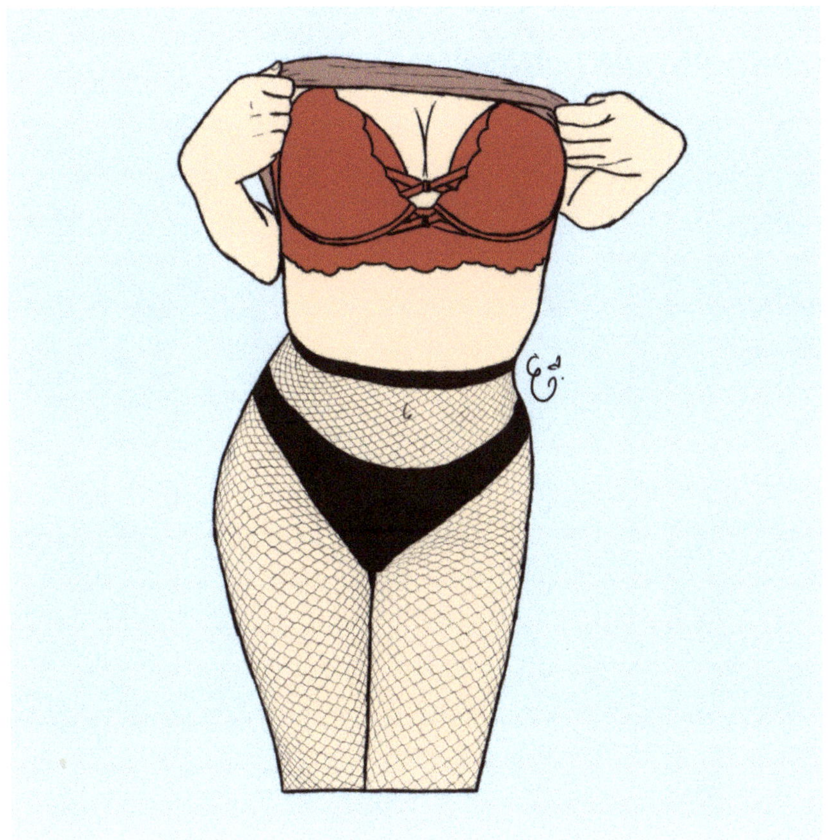

Brian L. Jacobs

San Francisco with the Fraternity Sisters 1991

at the Church of the Holy Phallus
a room was set aside for golden showers

and we buttfucked
hopefully

with AIDS on
periphery

1984 Toyota Celica

sewn into my fashion in Cypress on Valley View Blvd towards the 405
to Los Angeles where faggots drip down Melrose

flaming *Duran Duran* crimps and old punks cock stare
in the toilets of the *Odyssey* or *Peanuts*

where Nina Hagen begs *New York New York*
and Kate Gardner *Shiney Shineys*

and *Tin Tin* kisses me
a cypress tree gun

Rhizomes of My Refusals

amputate walking refusals hunted by artifice
arid mirrors rush at orts meat

icy an offal of rat touched loin
travel onerous conduits between languages

no intention resists the upsurge fantasy
illumination becomes stellated

fugitive triumphant escapes
writing the shadow of what will write

Global Tindering

"As stars with trains of fire and dews of blood,
Disasters in the sun; and the moist star…" William Shakespeare

it was in the lint in the laundry
between my vulva cracks

a ghost gone did it wrong
bivouacked in the middle of the Filchner-Ronne Ice Shelf

Peace Pilgrimage Ramadan February 1995lf

once I walked with Hamas
accidentally in their human forms

Claudio Parentela

Untitled

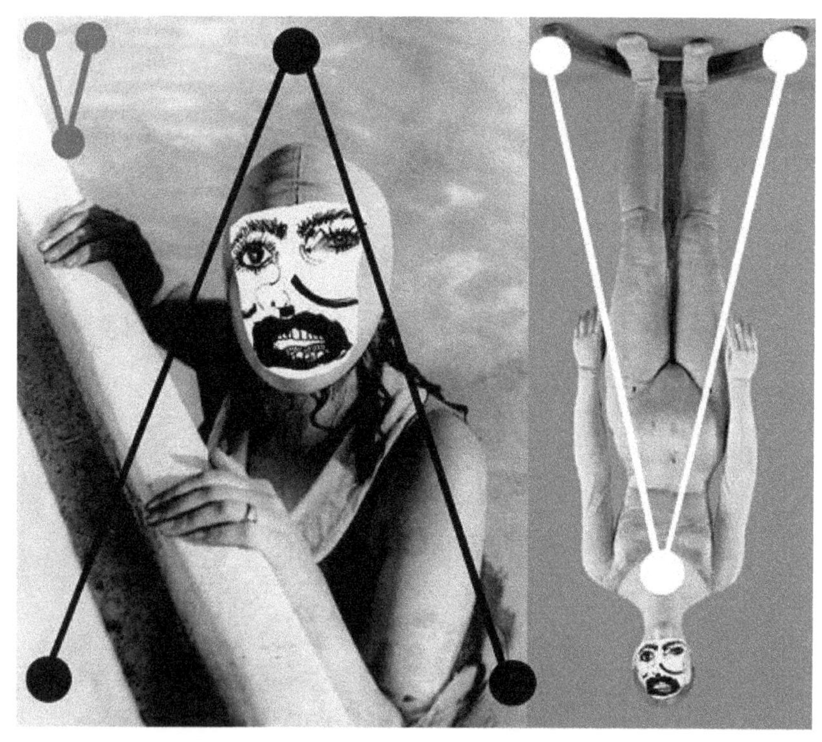

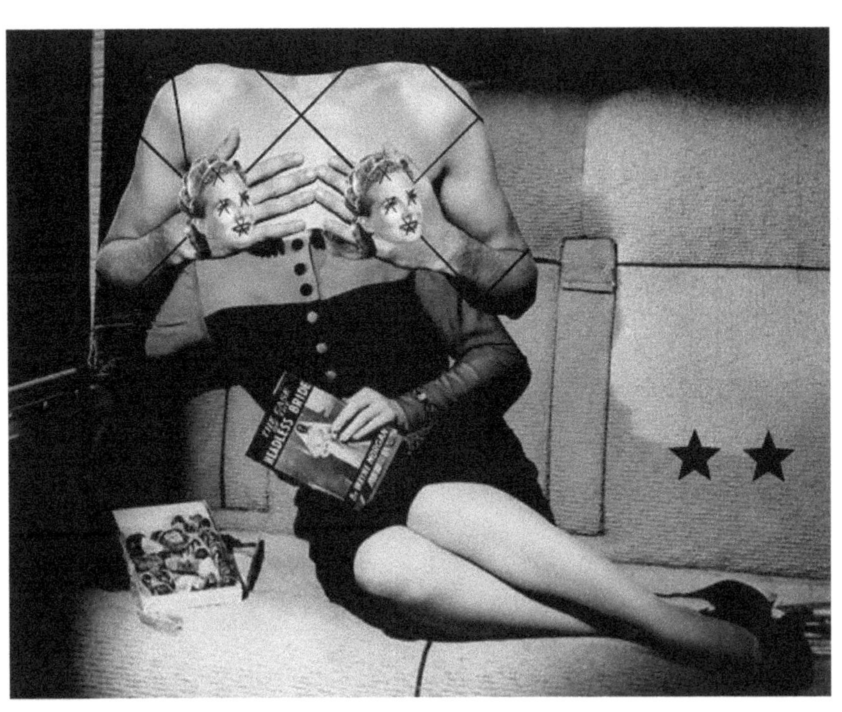
THE
HEADLESS BRIDE

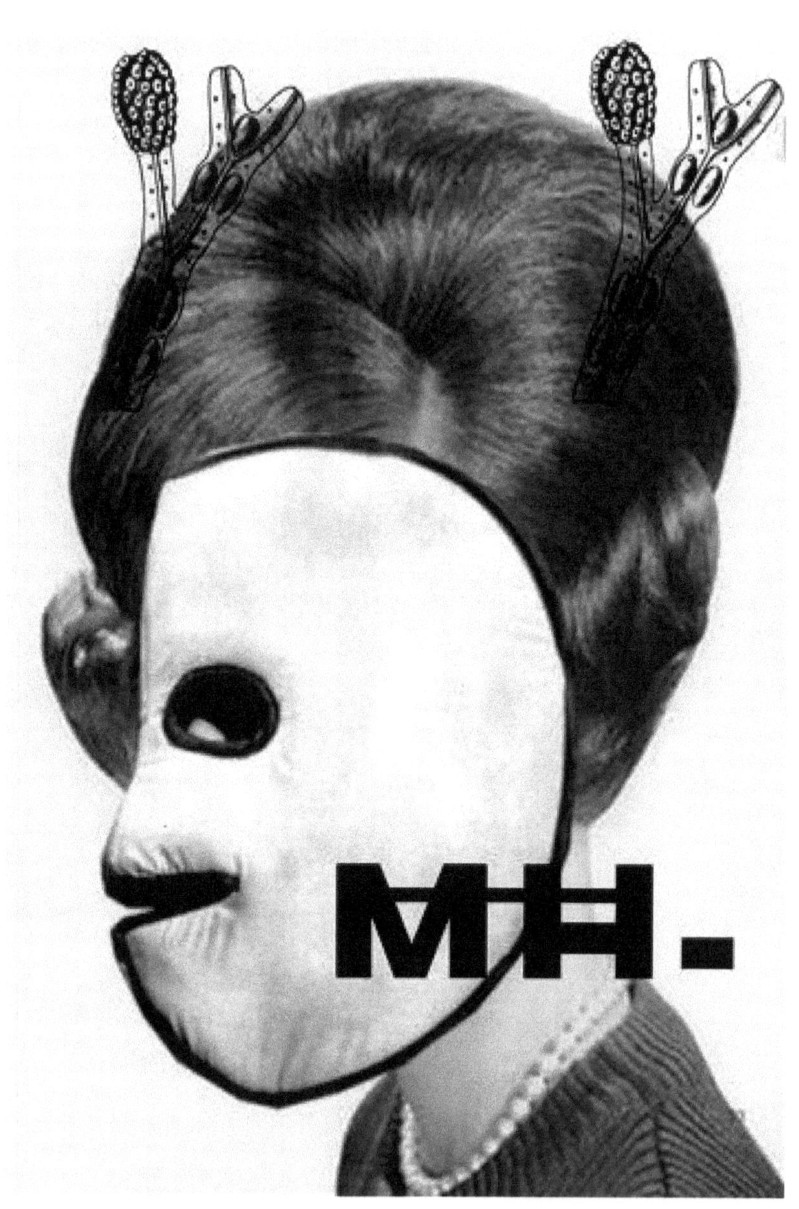
MH.

".^^
]]]%
%/&/

>>|||
*:
ooo
^^^
()

Jay Aelick

In Vienna

Even here, the dog's hair.
Already it lines my new apartment
seven thousand kilometers
from him. I shed it
from my sweaters, socks; sprinkle it
like a breadcrumb trail around the city.
This morning,
I walk a different route to work, careful
to wind the threads of him through every alley,
tying little bows around the lampposts.
When he comes, I want him to find himself
everywhere in this new place.
I want him to take in its scent
and know home.

for Ace and Coope

For City Pigeons.

Your one-note song needs no constructive criticism.
When you inhale, your chest swells into canvas, ambers
with sun. At home by default,
you have no need for nestbuilding; do it anyway
so that the other birds don't feel insecure.
Though you can't read, your flight
is the sound of a thousand pages turning
and many millennia wiser.
It's a crime I ever looked at you
and failed to notice the S-Bahn grime's calligraphy
scrawled along your wingtips, the drainwater sapphires
you carry on your back.
I wish there was no need to convince anyone of your beauty.
For a world where anyone who reads this nods along: *I know it.*

I know.

The Ace of Pentacles Responds

Sure, the arch in the hedge less arch itself than a reminder of the fact of a beyond.
And yes, the glint of mountain it reveals not unlike a Tarot card
onto which you could project a promise of anything, no, everything you'd ever need
to call yourself alive. Consider: even if you don't want everything, or even to be alive,
categorically, you want those lawn chairs, the kind with rubber slats that tease
at your leg hairs as you stand. You want the sparklers they sell out of the old firehouse,
the ones that burn too close to the base, blister the place between your forefinger
and thumb. You want to go barefoot; who cares if the summer's beer bottles still linger
around the honeysuckle at the edge of the yard, waiting to catch your soles off-guard?
There you are, seeing mountain and garden only permission to desire what they are not.
Look at me.
How I collapse the distance between arch and peak, between world as it is
and world as you'd have it into flat blue. If you let me, I can show you
a place where everything is so immensely itself, there's no need
for you to put yourself in any of it.

Melinda R. Smith

Works

I'm either seeing things
or I'm seeing things.

And?
So?

Gordon Blitz

Holy Hat

The bonnet separates
Me from a higher power
Wholly Holy
The sun eats away
At my head
Burning through hair follicles
Searching the scalp
Making a whole
On the top
Of my green hat
Sweating through
100% Algodon
Cotton threads
The aged cap
No longer protects
The epidermis
Failure of the
Brimming shield
Hides the cancerous
Rays
Spiriting me away

Shelley Stoehr

muscle memory

she was
a bodybuilder in another life well
it was this life well it is this life but also
a lifetime ago she started lifting weights
after she was attacked outside
the stop & shop late one night
by a roving gang of young men
so now when she finishes work
she goes to the bars until closing
after which she goes to the gym
where she pumps iron till nearly
sunrise bodybuilding ravages
her body so before she goes
to work tonight she'll get
a massage she likes to play
loud death-metal while she's
getting a massage because new-
age flutes and whale songs make
her anxious her massage therapist
digs into her rock-hard muscles
with an elbow and when it's
over she tips her massage
therapist with valium she
gets from a deli in the mission
district which is right next to
the castro where she'll go tonight
for halloween which is a raucous
event when the crowd is thick
with the costumed freaks
who are her people last year
she saw two men walking
in tandem with a replica
of the golden gate
bridge strung be-
tween them the best
part was that every
few feet they
would pause
and shake
like an
earth-
quake

Sam Heyd

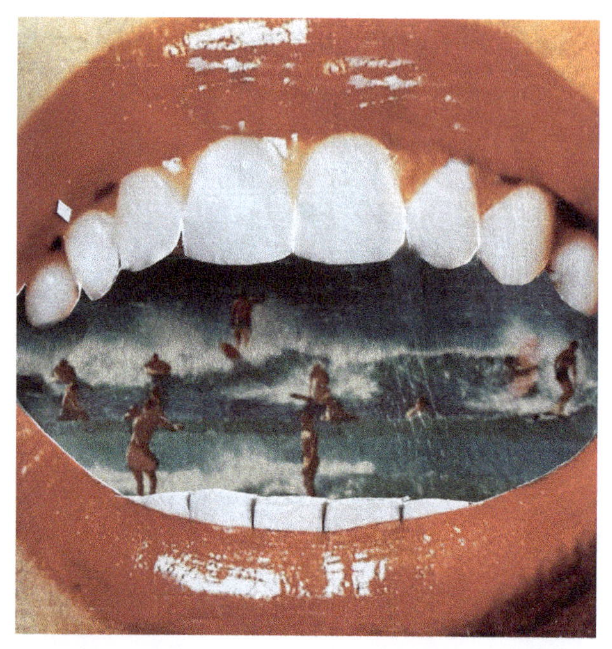

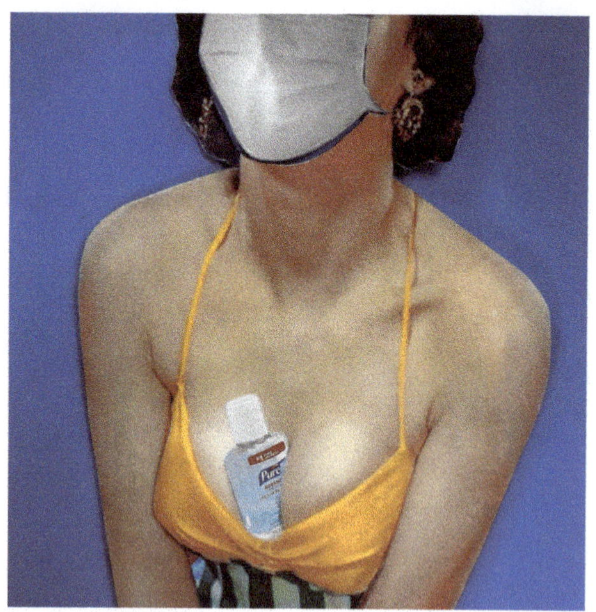

NATURAL COLOR PHOTOGRAPH

GOD IS Here

"the right to opaqueness"

-Glissant

Charlie Becker

How to Be Thin

For the sake
of being
pure
my sister
doesn't ever
eat
until
things
are under
control, her work
is done
everyone else
is happily
fed
and no one
is watching
her body
never stops
moving
calculating
always afraid
of an excess
others don't notice
but she
obsessively
shuns
my sister
skin

over bones
almost dies
in rehab
her profile
reduced
to ancient
war-torn
skull
until
finally
she is guided
to look
at herself
in a mirror, make
paper masks
of her face
and all
she can
see
is her
begging
smile.

Joelle Wilcock

Untitled

Sara E. Hughes

[the wake]

the spuds in the kitchen are
growing eyes at a rate i can neither
explain nor track. there are spores
on the bread and water is pooling
from the fridge. they say to pre
pare not for the weeks after the
funeral, but the months when the
fewer count the days.

in the evenings i forget how gin
tastes & hold my breath until i
remember. to be general, i want to
make this make sense. to be
specific, i will sound out a list of
animals like you starting with the
letter "g." some days i don't
make it past "giraffe" & fall asl
eep on the couch. i wait for so
meone to carry me to bed, &
when you do not come, i make a
glass of lemon water, so that i can
drink it.

Mary-Jo Okawa

Works

JP McGowan

My Dog Doesn't Answer Me When I Call Her

She used to, when I first got her. Everybody says Cudi is my dog, but she doesn't answer when I call her. They say that to be nice. I was allowed to get Cudi a couple months after I fed a hose from my exhaust pipe into my window, and they don't want me to do that again. I think it would've worked, but I was high and didn't know if it was the weed or exhaust making me so sleepy and if everyone had seen the hose I would've been really embarrassed. The punishment for failing to kill yourself is a week in a psychiatric ward where there's floor to ceiling windows overlooking a parking lot but you're still not allowed to go outside. I'd asked for a dog my whole life and they always said no, but when you're down in the dumps people will give you anything you ask for. I would've given myself carbon monoxide poisoning years ago if I knew that was all it took.

Cudi was my first rescue. Half Black Lab, half Australian Shepherd. She looks like a lab, except for the white spot on her chest that all Aussies have. She's got a lab temperament, too, but she runs like a shepherd. I don't like to run. My dad likes to run, because he quit drinking after my mom gave him an ultimatum. My dad was a lot of fun when he was still drinking—if he got drunk enough, he would talk in the Sling Blade voice and we would listen to the Grateful Dead together—but it's nice that he doesn't get angry anymore. It's embarrassing that my suicide gift doesn't enjoy spending time around me, doubly so, since the whole reason I was there in the first place was that nobody enjoyed spending time around me. People enjoy being around my dad. He converted to Catholicism when he married my mom which I don't think counts and neither does she, but everybody at church still likes him more than us.

My dad named me after him, so as long as he's around and sober, I'll be everyone's second favorite Jonathan Pope, including my dogs. 2ⁿᵈ place isn't bad, I got second place in a writing contest last year. First place was $500, and second place was a handshake. I think that sums it up.

It was snowing when I got Cudi, and she shivered the whole way home. She was wrapped in an old maroon blanket with fringe on the end and she pissed all over the blanket. She was scared of the hardwood floors in my living room and wouldn't leave the carpet that ties the room together. I didn't understand it, because it was a nice carpet when we got it, but at that point it was already old and faded. For the first three weeks she slept in my bed. At night, I would smoke weed with half of my body outside of my second-floor bedroom window and the other half on my bed. I was too scared to leave her all alone. She was so small and helpless back then; I'd never loved anything more. Then, my mom got a puppy, a cute little golden doodle who we call Rosie. Cudi and Rosie started to sleep in my parents' room. I was at school all day, so was my mom. My dad had just gotten laid off. He spent all day with them. I had lacrosse practice after school and that didn't end till 5, but most days I went and smoked weed with my friends and didn't get home until 8 or so. My parents didn't want me to smoke weed; I went straight to my room so they wouldn't notice. The dogs stayed downstairs. In high school, my parents left me home alone with the dogs one weekend. I had some friends over and we all did acid and Cudi hates acid, so when my friend didn't close the door, she walked away and I didn't notice for a while. She never forgave me.

I hope my dog loves me. She would definitely love me if my dad wasn't unemployed during the formative year of her life. He stole her from me. He gives her coconut oil and treats and bacon even though we all agreed not to. The other day my mom made a pork roast and he gave her the end slice—the best slice. That's cheating, in my book. I bet my mom felt like this when they raised kids together. But the worst part about the treats is they make her fat. Not that being fat is an issue, but older labs are known to have hip problems, and I don't want her to have that. My Grandma has a bum hip, and I see how much it bothers her. My dad knows that Cudi is his dog now, and I think he's proud of that too. That's okay, I would be too if it was me and not him, but it's not, so I'm not. My dad loves to go to the park. He was born before Twitter and Instagram so the dogs don't look at him like they look at me when I'm on my phone. They get excited when he opens the garage door because they know that he'll take them running at the park. I take them too, but they won't go if he's at home. When I come home, my dad will tell Cudi "there's Jonathan, go say Hi to Jonathan," but she doesn't. He's throwing it in my face. Sober people have a superiority complex.

The other day, I whistled for my dogs when I was going to the garage. Rosie came running because she loves me, Cudi followed behind, probably out of curiosity. I tried to turn the garage light on but the ceiling fixture in the kitchen turned off—I guess I had it backwards. In the garage, I went over to the work bench where I keep my bong in a big red bucket so it's not so obvious. There's a wood sign that one of my sisters nailed the letters D-A-D into as a gift that sits on top of it. Rosie came and laid on top of my feet. Cudi laid down against the steps. When I opened the door to let her back in, she held her head straight except her eyes stayed on me the whole time. She was judging me, but at least she didn't say anything mean.

Rosie is a therapy dog. My mom takes her to work at the high school, and she puts her paws on the barn door of my mom's office as the students walk by. Rosie knows when she has work to do because they put a big red vest on her that says I AM A THERAPY DOG. I don't think my mom ever taught her how to read, but the vest still works. I get sad a lot at home, and I want to cuddle with my dogs, but my mom doesn't let them get on the couch. Sometimes I'll lay on Cudi, but she hates the smell of weed and she almost always gets up and goes to the other room. The last time I was home, I put the vest on Rosie. At least then she would feel obligated to be nice to me. Anyways, with the whole work from home revolution I figured she might like a change of pace. She did good, but I could tell she saw me as a client, not a friend. Later that day I tried to put the vest on Cudi, but she just ripped it off.

I'm gone a lot. Even when I was living at home, I was gone a lot, but now I'm only at home a few weeks out of the year. I could take Cudi with me, but that would be selfish. Every time I come back, I weigh a little less, my face doesn't look quite the same as before. I usually have a new haircut, new clothes and new shoes. I've got new friends and new opportunities.

Pretty soon, I'll be living in a new place with a new job surrounded by new people. I wish that I could come home, and it is all the same as it was when I was seventeen, but it's not. I wish I was the same as I was when I was seventeen, but I'm not. Maybe my dog doesn't answer me when I call her because she doesn't recognize me, the person I am today. That would be better than her not answering when I call her because she doesn't like me. But I would understand, I feel the same way honestly. Maybe I could get sober or exercise or apologize to the people I've hurt, like my Dad did, but I don't want to copy him. We already have the same name. Plus, it seems kind of played out. Still, it would be nice if she would get in my bed again sometime when I was sleeping—I moved my mattress to the floor so it would be easier for her to get in—but she won't. My sheets are nice, but my dads' have a higher thread count.

J'han Brady

Acclimation

Matt Hollrah

Once Again

The chickens celebrate another egg.
        The cowpen daisies are in frantic bloom,
yellow petals visible half a mile away.

The walnut moth caterpillars fall from trees,
        like fuzzy eyebrows of old men,
and someone is killing doves in a neighboring field.

My dog browses the barnyard
        for morsels of cow manure,
while the nation whips itself into a frenzy
        over what can be said
after one radical murders another.

The owls are exactly what they seem
        and hoot to each other across the acres,
signaling their presence without being seen.

I've lost a contest, one I had a chance to win,
        and weary of competition,
while a hummingbird visits every tiny blossom
        of lantana exploding with pink and yellow.

I must remind myself once again
        of what happens without ego

The World Before Phones

There were long stretches
full of silence and sitting and solitude.
Strange, I know, but people
looked straight ahead. Their eyes
always pointed forward,
parallel to the ground.
When we went to the bathroom,
we just went. We didn't also shop for pants.
Nobody took pictures of their food,
and we used irony all the time
without fear of misunderstanding.
We'd gather in uninterrupted
conversation, so engrossed
that our minds would lock together
like Legos, would meld like
balls of Silly Putty, shaped
by the sheer joy of human contact.

Often, one of us would ask,
"What is the capital of Mozambique?"
and someone would say, "I don't know."
We'd have to start asking around,
and no one would know, so we'd
all say, "Let's ask John. John will
know." And others would say,
"No, John doesn't know capitals.
Let's ask Cathy. She's better at that."
But Cathy was away traveling,
and you couldn't call—it was before phones—

so you'd just have to wait for Cathy
to get back. Always, there was
someone who didn't want to wait.
They would drive for hours
to this place with stacks and stacks
of books piled on each other,
containing nothing but lists
of the names of cities, and if the city
was a capital, it had an asterisk,
and that's how you'd know.
That way, or asking Cathy
when she got back.

Of course, a really long time before phones,
you had to go to Mozambique
to find out the capital of Mozambique,
and we would land at the coastal village
and ask, "Is this the capital of Mozambique?"
And they would say, "No, it's farther on,
Keep going." So we would walk
some more, and at the next town
we'd ask again, "Is this the capital of Mozambique?"
And the people would say, "No, no,
it's farther on." And we'd end up on
the opposite coast and ask again, "Is this the capital of Mozambique?"

and the people on the opposite coast
with the harbor called Sandwich,
where they sold us marula and jackalberry
but no sandwiches, would say,

"No, no. This is Namibia.
You passed it miles back on your way in."
So we backtracked, but often people
there didn't know either where the capital was
or what a capital was or what an asterisk was.

"we used irony all the time without fear of misunderstanding"

Mario Loprete

Carrie Cantalupo

riding on the back of a bee

the scent of orange, bergamot intoxicant
pollen clinging to our legs

fumble through stamen
rub and strum

shed semen, hard to hold
onto his excitement

diaphanous wings
fanning furiously

a slight irritation
of weight

but good natured
about my drag

after a long floral frenzy
we linger in buttercup

a woman with a crooked wig

sits by her self in the booth
drinks chocolate milk with a straw
reads an old People magazine
doesn't jump when a tray of dishes is dropped
her skin is yellow

the waitress sets down my salad
follows my gaze
"She doesn't have cancer. She has bad hair."

I am relieved
but disappointed, too
I didn't get the story right

at Meijer
an old lady in line wears a babushka
over pink foam curlers
carries a flowered cloth purse
tells a chicken joke to the cashier
leans heavily on her cart
has two cases of Ensure

she must be going home to take care of her husband
a man who does not remember her

The cashier takes her money
says, "See you and your old man at the casino tonight"
pulling down on an imaginary handle

I am relieved
but disappointed, too
I didn't get this one right, either

and I am the woman looking at her reflection in the window
looking for lipstick on her teeth
waiting for something big to happen
wondering if this is the story she has in her head?

"Flying Gardens of Maybe"

inspired by A.S. Yang

where a seed lands
hard scrabble or silt
rain drenched or dry
daisies, coreopsis
take root
sprout
vines trumpet songs
so colorful eyes tingle

wind swept or
bird droppings
seeds become
rapt possibility
an ecology of chance

love, too, a kernel
can germinate
in cracks and crevices
an alchemy nudged
with a puff of air
errant rain

it's so miraculous
all of it
the randomness of nature
a haphazard symmetry
with little rhyme or reason

all while ants traipse by
and birds take baths
in puddles
all just a maybe

Marl Meier

Untitled

Jones Irwin

Deep Image or A Painting by Jeffrey Dahmer

Is it true that Jerome Rothenberg
came up with the concept of 'deep image'
after he wilfully opened a large pomegranate in his kitchen
and the blood splattered across the four walls
like a painting by Jeffrey Dahmer?

Turner's Ghost

At Cotter Force where
Turner sketched the children
looking down at him from
the six-step waterfall the
sun comes back out midday
to warm the sweet vernal grass.
It is Saturday mid-August as we
drive back through Swaledale the
Cow House with the two red doors
the open windows where the children
pushed the hay for flattening inside.
The rooks and the sheep seem intimates
round these parts as if in concert between
the surrounding Muker hills. The swirling rain
will be back soon so let's head for the *Green
Dragon Inn* as fast as we can so we can talk again
to Turner's ghost and ask him if those wild
childers up and down the six steps perturbed
or inspired his sketch of this Yorkshire dark pool.

A Beautiful Woman

She truly was a beautiful woman
with a mouth that immediately gave one ideas
her hazel eyes with green highlights
and her long legs and designer jeans suggested that indeed
Gallo Barcetta an ageing widower with a taste for younger girls
may have felt the need to be extra generous in this specific case

But it was nonetheless difficult to imagine
that this elegant and subtle beauty named Giovanna
could have been capable of shooting a bullet through the back
of Gallo's neck as he sat drinking coffee at the breakfast table
coming out the nose taking with it one eye and part of the forehead
although it was clear that the night before Gallo did not sleep alone
and that several strands of long blonde hair had been found on the
pillow by Forensics
which at first glance seemed to match those of Giovanna
who to the contrary claimed to have spent the night with her husband
in Vigata

She truly was a beautiful woman
with a mouth that immediately gave one ideas

At Catania

I find myself again
mid-January
when the Fish Market
is not as crowded as May
and the artichoke barbeques
have more space for their fire and smoke

Reading Pasolini as always here
yesterday I gave a talk on Freire at the University
and the crowd wondered aloud
whether we could recreate the Sixties counter-culture
once more in Sicily and elsewhere
or whether simply it was now too late for that?

The Death of Poe
After Artaud
If Poe was found dead one morning
in an alleyway in Baltimore, it was not
because of his obvious alcoholism
but simply because of an army of
his enemies (scum!) who couldn't cope
with his beauty and had to take fatal
revenge on his poetry. I cannot forgive
these homiciders. Through their dastardly
crime, they prevented the poor world
from experiencing the heavy voodoo which
pulses through his work like a heartbeat. Thankfully,
he had translated Baudelaire before the vengeful got to his genius.
Or is that the other way around? And as his tortured body lay
dying in the Baltimore gutter, the spirit of French Symbolism
visited him and gave him the last rites.

The Unconscious is Structured as Yugoslavia
On the track from Dubrovnik to Herzegovina Sigmund
struggled to remember the name 'Signorelli' which set
off another train of associations through Turkey and Dalmatia
in this elliptical Austro-Hungarian citizen's mind concerning
the Balkans as the Unconscious of Europe a place that must
be suppressed at all costs or else forgotten things and the most
shameful missed opportunities plus secrets of sexuality and death
would return and come back to bite you full blast on the ass

Letter from Laure to Georges Bataille #1
Dear Georges,
Our connection, once so strong, now hangs by the most fragile thread.
I have been looking at the clock all day, it tick tocks so loud in this cold
room and it is fully six hours now and you still haven't rang me.
Honestly, I tell you, you absolute bastard, that if you do not phone me
within the next ten minutes, that everything between us is finally over.
I know you have probably spent the whole afternoon fucking another
woman who is not me, giving each other mutual bodily pleasures. How
exactly do you think that this makes me feel? I don't mean to be
malicious. I know that you are a whore. That won't change.
I'm allowing you one last chance. Ten minutes, actually it is now nine.
[clock ticking loudly]
You bastard. You make me want to hire a Bulgarian hit squad.
But I must remain strong. You will never break me. And, if necessary,
I will break you, Georges.
Laure

My Hands Are A City

My hands are a city, say Thessaloniki
They caress my burning face in the afternoon blaze
Yesterday was 34 today is even hotter
On the public bus we are all intimates
My hands reach out to an old man who is weeping
My hands cup his tears like a chalice
He says *efcharisto* but his lament is continuous

For Bela Lugosi #1

After David Meltzer
Bela, when you say
Transylvania or *Goth*
Or
I am Count Dracula
You sound exactly like Peter Murphy
Which is frankly uncanny
And chronologically surreal

It is hardly a surprise then
That you were also a junkie

Neither of you were ever
Called assholes even though
You both drifted into myriad bedrooms
Taking your clothes off
And pretending it was Art

Bela even drank blood
From women's necks
And got away with it

The Boy From Tunbridge Wells
i.m. Shane Mac Gowan

What kind of errant boy
Gets born in Kent
Only to end up
In a wooden casket
Stops the traffic
In a central Dublin street
A rainy December day
Pulled by black horses
With feather boa headdress
And IRA freedom songs
From out their gritted teeth
To send him off to death
A carriage driver in a top hat

What kind of crazy boy is that?

The Holy Words of Tristan Tzara
After Jerome Rothenberg
Logic is always wrong
logic is always a death-knell
so get on your hobby horse
cries Dada
cries Tzara the Archangel
and forget about conscience
and forget about evil

for the good is the Devil

Rothenberg Haiku #1
Dada got Zurich
Dingdong went Kaput
Where Lenin sat

Housmans Bookshop Haiku
No to gentri-catastrophe
Books have soul at London
King's Cross – not for sale

Martello Tower, Portmarnock
A circular plan circa 1805
With a 1970 frontal extension
I run past you most weeks
In a breathless celebration

Follow your track down
To the Velvet Strand
In winter the high waves threaten
And yet you always remain serene

Stony silent and indignant
Like I'd imagine a Stoic philosopher
Should and would respond say Epictetus
The former slave to a world gone insane

Some Books Change Your Life

After T.S. Eliot

Some books change your life
As in December 1908 in his junior year
At Harvard Eliot took down from the shelves
The Symbolist Movement in Literature by Symons Arthur

Not unlike Joyce in Dublin University
Who devoured it in the early century
Which packed him off to Paris
So as to discover French literature

And then there was Francis Bacon in London
Painting the agonies of the Tryptich of Sweeney
Under the influence of our American poet in turn
Bringing outrageous paintings into light
As if ice was fiery again by the tutelage of sun

Psychic Geography Haiku

A Burroughs-like
paranoid sense
of universal conflagration

A flood of 2020s
documentary nonfiction
neo-gothic A-Z of London

As if we were all
dining on stones and hashish
chasing post-Beat poetics

A character called Undark
secreting an occult text
under a long grey cloak

Spotted on Holloway Road
stood outside *Ram Books*
rhyming obscene lines

An earlier career book
dealing replaced by Tarot
as stealthier in the Underworld

And wealthier by far
although Lucifer will look
for payback from all clients

Reader, I kid you not
just note the sorry fate
of Jack 'The Hat' Mc Vitie

Tragic Optimism
With Char, we can see
The world in ruins
Destruction by our own minds
Or hands
As with the two traitors he
Had to execute as part
Of leading the Resistance
Whilst knowing that this
Would come back to haunt
And yet to continue to create
To see your own soul as a double
Often acting even against itself
To accept your responsibility
To seek to own up to your innermost bad faith
Whilst remaining optimistic that there is a path
To write

Portrait de Madeleine Riffaud

After a drawing by Picasso, November 1944

At just nineteen
You shot and killed a Nazi
Near *Le Louvre*

Arrested and tortured
You escaped the *Gestapo*
By jumping a train

Once again they recaptured you
Sentenced you to death
But the Liberation was just as abrupt

On August 19, 1944
You reentered Paris
A free woman

In Picasso's *The Clenched Fist*
We see your courageous face
Your long black hair is your valour

Beat Hotel Haiku #1

At 9 Rue Gît-le-Coeur
Spot Rimbaud in a raincoat
Ginsberg vomiting Apollinaire

My Hands Are A City

My hands are a city, say Thessaloniki
They caress my burning face in the afternoon blaze
Yesterday was 34 today is even hotter
On the public bus we are all intimates
My hands reach out to an old man who is weeping
My hands cup his tears like a chalice
He says *efcharisto* but his lament is continuous

Student Revolt Thessaloniki Haikus
I interviewed Alexis
Who told me about riots
    -    against the privatised University

At Aristotle Thessaloniki
Anarchists stage an occupation
    -    no to commercial education

Students repainted *Guernica*
To avoid the same fate
    -    it hangs in the Rectorate

AntiCapitalists gather in the Steki
Iced coffee for the Revolution
    -    caffeine helps with enlightenment

In the city it hits 38 degrees
The Gaza demo does Aristotelous
    -    black and red flags rise

Petros sees an uncertain future
Tales of hurt and of exploitation
    -    oppression without redemption

Together we read Kropotkin
Later Marx and Bakunin
    -    literature is a burning sun

Aliki thinks I'm mad
To think this at Halkidiki
    -    student revolt will win out

Lucien #1

'a specifically English art'
Freud said that you needed
a complete knowledge of life
in order to make a painting of life
as the religious adoration of life
puts awe in between reality and paint
which stops you from examining it
which stops you from daring to change it

which explains the short-lived nature of
his two marriages and his numerous affairs
as he never allowed himself to
succumb to religious awe

Instead, he employed an excruciatingly
deliberate technique where he would
focus obsessively on the physical details
of each sitter, day and night
in this way the truth would slowly always come out
always come out into the stark and unforgiving light

Using hog-hair brushes enabled a paint that was thicker and more
aggressive
highlighting imperfection in the skin of his sitters
as well as the more subtle effects of light and shade on the skin's surface
where the face is merely a limb and cannot provide the complete
portrait
where body portraits in a splayed or contorted position
on beds, sofas or piles of dirty old rags
imbue the work with an authentic emotionalism

Suicide Bridge #1

What have the dwellings
of Blake and Keats got to do
with the malevolent spirits of
modern England if not clearly
delineated in detective work concerning
what was indeed thrown off *Suicide Bridge*
so as to dump evidence concerning the murder
of Jack 'the Hat' Mc Vitie in and around the 1970s
by none other than the very *Kray Gang* themselves?

Moreover, the coming to power in 1979 of
the Conservative government is no coincidence here
and you don't have to be an Irish soothsayer to call out
the 'autistic poses' of the *Sons of Albion* as offering a
portentous warning of what would happen next.

Autobiographia Literaria
After Frank O'Hara
When I was a child
I often went to my
father's home in Sligo
and played in the rough backyard

I loved Action Men and then
later Punk music and as a teenager
I sold vinyl in the city

If anyone told me to read
aloud I asked the next person to
be chosen, saying 'I am not yet born'

And here I am today, battle-weary,
writing this poetry, my own.
Imagine!

Black Mountain Haiku #1
No bullshit school
More Charlie Parker
Sax life

#D.T. Suzuki Haiku
Met Kerouac Fall '58
Red flush face
Advised green tea

Marilyn With Canvas Haiku #1
Blonde goddess
No screen
Only paint

“More Charlie Parker”

Andrew Lincoln Nelson

AutoEuryalideaBorg, 2023, Graphite on Strathmore Series 500 Bristol board, 25.5" x 34"

Dynaflorg One, 2024, Graphite on Strathmore Series 500 Bristol board, 25.5" x 34"

MolluscaBorg, 2025, Graphite on Strathmore Series 500 Bristol board, 25.5" x 34"

Chris Hamel

Sad

A simple word
Accessible to all
Simple to say and spell
An effortless lesson
For a child

In the writing
The serpentine *S*
Is the challenge
A line that sways
Back and forth
And crawls both
Up and down
The *a* and the *d*
Simple spheres
Carrying flagpoles
Of different length

In the saying
The tongue is key
Pressing gently
Against front teeth
Contorting enough
To allow the hiss
Of spent air
Its escape
Before the short *a*
Calls from the hall

Back in the throat
Telling the tongue
To kiss the palate
As *d* has come
To complete the job

Happy is more complex
Two syllables
Divided at the *p*'s
Foolish duplication
Nearly no sound
But an exhale of *h*
And the popping
Of the lips
Kissing each other
Followed by the *y*
The joyful sound
Of two *ee*'s
Making friends

Sad is simple
Like a farmer
With much to do
Grief requires tending
No time for tricks
Or linguistic games
Asking only that
As she busies herself
With our hurting hearts
That we step aside
And let her do her work.

Twelve Line Disciples with Jesus and Mary

Some poets I read
Many actually
Write their poems
By hand
With pens
And at times
A Blackwing pencil
In notebooks
Or maybe on
A yellow legal pad
In the cursive script
Of my mother's hand

20th Century people
Reading a 21st Century page

Some of those poets
Just a few I think
Can extract the essence
The very soul
Of nearly any moment
Seeing past all form
Not distracted
By the crisp
And cartoonishly long
Shadow
Cast by the sun
Of a late summer day

Visionaries I suppose
Like Blake and Bukowski

And there are poets
Only a couple really
Who say the words
To the songs we sing
When we are not
Thinking
Lost as we are
In the staccato tap
That quick sound
Of prancing fingers
On a ghost blue
Alphabet dance floor

Spelling our names
And the names of the dead

A Book of Essays

I want to write a book of essays
Not poetry
Not stories
Not a novel
I want to write something real.

There's the unraked leaves from
My neighbor's yard,
Piling in uncountable numbers
On my treeless lot.
The uninvited work
To gather them
While pushy Northern winds
Giggle at the mischief.
My back burning in ache
My mind burning
In Puritanical judgment
Of the *Polis* code betrayed.
Is this real?

Here a colleague
Whose abject absence
Of initiative and industry
Is truly a marvel.
Directing his appointed affairs
From a reclined chair,
Bag of popcorn in his hand
Chomping on kernels
While he asks cynically

About the staff meeting
From which he was excused
Because of his appointed affairs
Which he performed
From a reclined chair
With a bag of popcorn
In his hand.
Is this real?

Or the dead children
From bombings far away
Victims of the new dictators
Voted into office
By fear taught minds
Whose eyes see some,
But can't look past
Their inflated
Cornfed bellies
To catch even a glimpse
Of the stained and misshapen
Crocs worn
On their diabetic feet,
Feet which would fail them
If they were forced to run
From the falling bombs
Dropped by the new dictator

Who, too, is afraid.
Is this real?

Maybe the game of football
Glory vain and infectious
Maiming as it does
The bodies of hoodwinked boys
And the souls
Of cowards
Who gather in crowds
To cheer jeer and leer
Unable to hear
The crack of a breaking bone
Or the cries of the vanquished
Which really is all of us.
Acolytes
Conquered by blood lust
And the tribal urges
Which justify themselves.
Is this real?

"The bodies of hoodwinked boys And the souls Of cowards"

Samantha R. Sharp

How to Give a Lecture

my skirt   my gut
excruciating   palpitating
                bloated
        inflated   hot
stamped   static
folder/name/date/kind   signed
dual factor   press rewind   play
every day I want to know   would the lights still burn
                        if the circuit   wound logic
                                to sense?
Did we have a   n i c e
                        n i c e , l o n g
project protract   proctor
pesticide   w e e k e n d ?
glassy mass   razorthin   starry
rotoscope version   of us   pen
hold   scan   bite
On page three,
        tv screens lull
we   see   f i g u r e t w e l v e .
        me but not
spreading
        thousands
our spines   shake loose leather straps s
warm the vents
                go under   ground
bloom in grass where bellflowers   bend down   dust

noses   erase
each other   like chalk
                 til bulbs of artificial light
W h o r e m e m b e r s   the difference between reemerge
                            almost
                    a s u b j e c t a n d   a n   o b j e c t ?
             as transparent   as
to stifle

noise holed up   in my belly and tongue   my belly
                tongue
to be   killed   by
pastel cardigans skirts how   how could this be if,   if   I
said   the
                words right?

Jessica G. de Koninck

Le Journal de la Beauté

(John Rhead Louis, 1897, [Leonard A. Lauder Collection of American
Posters at the Metropolitan Museum of Art])

Beauty is for sale the peacocks teach. Vain birds,
for ten cents they spread their feathered tails,

reveal a thousand purple eyes, flecked with green and blue,
that spill across the daisied fields as if for your pleasure,

not theirs. They use their fiery bodies to seduce,
to compel you to follow the twisted dirt road. Where

do you think the path heads, this maze that spins you,
fills your blue heart with longing and regret?

You will spend a lifetime walking only to find he path
leads to the edge of the canvas and a stiff wooden frame.

Jennifer Handy

Desperate Creatures

The sun is in league with Mother Nature, bleaching out all unnatural color.

I string a clothesline between a mesquite tree and one they call a crucifixion thorn.

The latter tree is rare, an endangered species in California, a place full of Messiahs.

A single dead mesquite leaf, I soon discover, will discolor anything white or pastel colored.

One evening around the summer solstice, something subtle shifts.

A bee appears upon my laundry, hearing perhaps the gentle noise of linen garments becoming stiff.

I sit inside, smearing calamine lotion on a heat rash spreading across my stomach.

I hear the buzzing of the bee. Then another and another.

By the time I go outside, there is a full-on swarm. My clothes are barely visible on the clothesline.

Somewhere along the way, the water situation went from low to critical. The bees gorge themselves on water.

Why don't you use a Laundromat, my mother asks me on the phone.

I make soap from olive oil and ashes. I use unchlorinated water.

The bees finally leave sometime after sunset. The rest of the season, I hang my clothes outside at night.

For weeks after the swarm, the bees return, furiously seeking water. I can sense their anger.

I leave water in a bucket some distance off, but somehow they never find it.

The vehicles attract them. They shine like running water.

Later, I make another try at hanging laundry up by day, staying beside it to watch for bees.

The only insect is a large black beetle with broken wings, one gone entirely, the other a mangled sheet of hammered copper, translucent and paper-thin.

During Covid, they shut off the water fountains at rest areas and public parks.

The rich have indoor plumbing and don't think twice about buying bottled water.

The homeless are like the beetle, living in the desert scrub land, scrounging for water that drips down upon a rock.

There is nothing I can do except to leave the dripping sheet.

I taste the bubbling amber sap of a nearby palo verde tree, supposedly edible, and find it bitter.

I stay and offer up my company to the dying beetle.

"string a clothesline between a mesquite
tree and one they call a crucifixion thorn"

George L Stein

Vogue

Bushwick

shoegaze++

(Don't be) jealous

Saint Mishima of the NE Corridor Line

Katie Cloutte

Visual Erasure

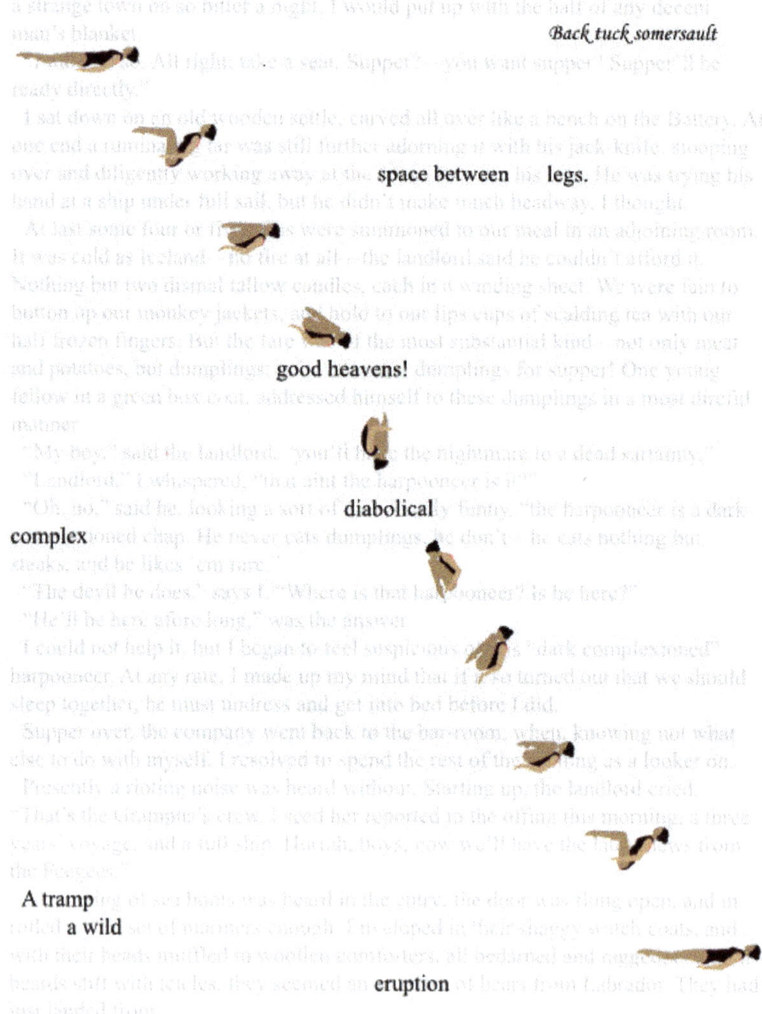

a strange town on so bitter a night. I would put up with the half of any decent man's blanket.

Back tuck somersault

 All right; take a seat. Supper?—you want supper? Supper'll be ready directly."

I sat down on an old wooden settle, carved all over like a bench on the Battery. At one end a ruminating tar was still further adorning it with his jack-knife, stooping over and diligently working away at the **space between** his **legs.** He was trying his hand at a ship under full sail, but he didn't make much headway, I thought.

At last some four or five of us were summoned to our meal in an adjoining room. It was cold as Iceland—no fire at all—the landlord said he couldn't afford it. Nothing but two dismal tallow candles, each in a winding sheet. We were fain to button up our monkey jackets, and hold to our lips cups of scalding tea with our half frozen fingers. But the fare was of the most substantial kind—not only meat and potatoes, but dumplings; **good heavens!** dumplings for supper! One young fellow in a green box coat, addressed himself to these dumplings in a most direful manner.

"My boy," said the landlord, "you'll have the nightmare to a dead sartainty."

"Landlord," I whispered, "that aint the harpooneer is it?"

"Oh, no," said he, looking a sort of **diabolical**ly funny, "the harpooneer is a dark **complex**ioned chap. He never eats dumplings, he don't—he eats nothing but steaks, and he likes 'em rare."

"The devil he does," says I. "Where is that harpooneer? Is he here?"

"He'll be here afore long," was the answer.

I could not help it, but I began to feel suspicious of this "dark complexioned" harpooneer. At any rate, I made up my mind that if it so turned out that we should sleep together, he must undress and get into bed before I did.

Supper over, the company went back to the bar-room, when, knowing not what else to do with myself, I resolved to spend the rest of the evening as a looker on.

Presently a rioting noise was heard without. Starting up, the landlord cried, "That's the Grampus's crew. I seed her reported in the offing this morning; a three years' voyage, and a full ship. Hurrah, boys, now we'll have the latest news from the Feegees."

A tramping of sea boots was heard in the entry; the door was flung open, and in rolled **a wild** set of mariners enough. Enveloped in their shaggy watch coats, and with their heads muffled in woollen comforters, all bedarned and ragged, and their beards stiff with icicles, they seemed an **eruption** of bears from Labrador. They had just landed from

Morgan Stone

MORNING

I have gone to the ocean to play
lift algae slick stones barnacle burnished
quick hand to catch tiny crabs burrow below
how the rock doesn't crush them—I wonder
when my 7-year-old fingers sometimes do
harried rush, closed fist, dump in my clear bucket
left on the shadowless balcony naked in the sun
under seagull caws, overlooking sea freedom
always dead by morning

I have gone to the ocean to heal
when I was broken like the crabs
under someone else's hand, longing
for a rock as heavy as the Atlantic to protect me
when I was boiled like the crabs overlooking sea
freedom through window pane glass bucket prison
but I, unlike the crabs fought to find the ocean
before floating supine to the surface
in morning

I have gone to the ocean to play
wary feet prod slimy tidal bay sand
diligent to avoid overturning sheltering rocks
my son raking mud, listen to the scrape
metal prongs drag on clam shell ridges
"I think I found one!"
a smile, proud, unveils rake from silted sea
monstrous crab, splayed, skewered through the belly
writhing legs, shock and pain—my son and crab
broken
back to the ocean we go
mourning

THE WAY OF THE RASPBERRIES

She was the raspberries
that grew in her backyard
spines and thorns
meticulously cared for and then one day
gone—hacked to the ground
"no one visits me so no one gets the raspberries"
mourning the tiny red drops of fruit
perhaps the way she mourned her husband
the shrapnel was inoperable
she found him hanging in the garage
open doors to the garden
my tongue still tastes the
syrup she would make
oozing from the glass bottle onto vanilla ice cream
blood red against the cream
the only sweetness that lingered
after she followed the way
of the raspberries

CEMETERY HOUSE

He felt bad about beating the baseball bat
into the alligator's head but it kept coming back
why didn't it just go away?
it just kept coming and "I wanted to see
what would happen."
I let him defend himself even though
no one was criticizing
politely listening, conceptualizing Houma,
Louisiana and beating an alligator
with a baseball bat from the hand
of this gentle man
who lay next to me one night in his bed
during a thunderstorm that shook
the walls of the tiny house next to the cemetery
I didn't want to be alone, he made sure
not to let even a toe fall astray too close to me
he dumps crawfish from an old
scarred red bucket onto the coffee table
a pile of orange and crimson legs and
antennae and eyeballs staring blankly
even as he tears the heads free
slurps the brain from shell
I eat his meat sauce from a mug, feet neatly tucked
under me on the couch while he sucks skulls
"Morgan, that's for pasta…"
but there is no pasta so

I keep eating it with my spoon assessing the lumps
made by gentle hands, suspended in red
and thinking of that poor alligators head

Rex Wilder
Eve and Adam

Now You

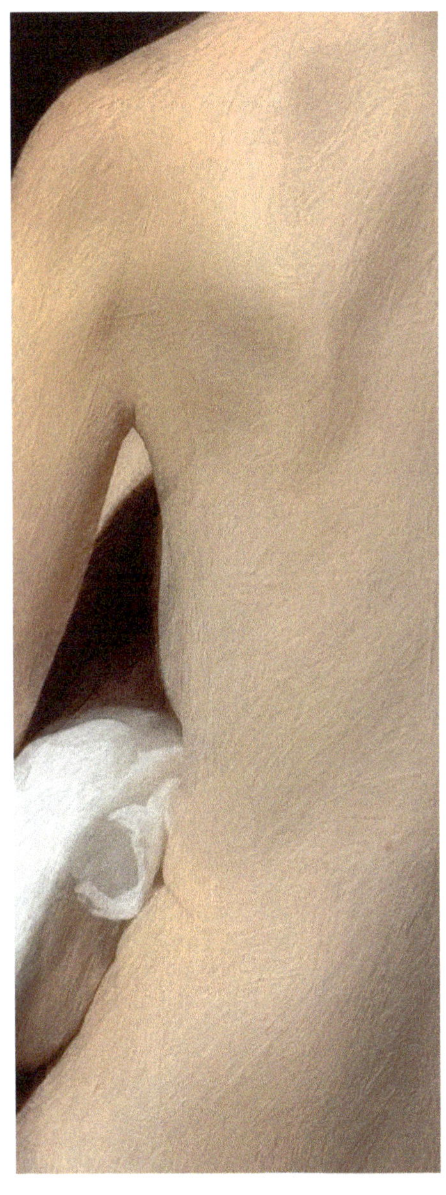

Forbidden

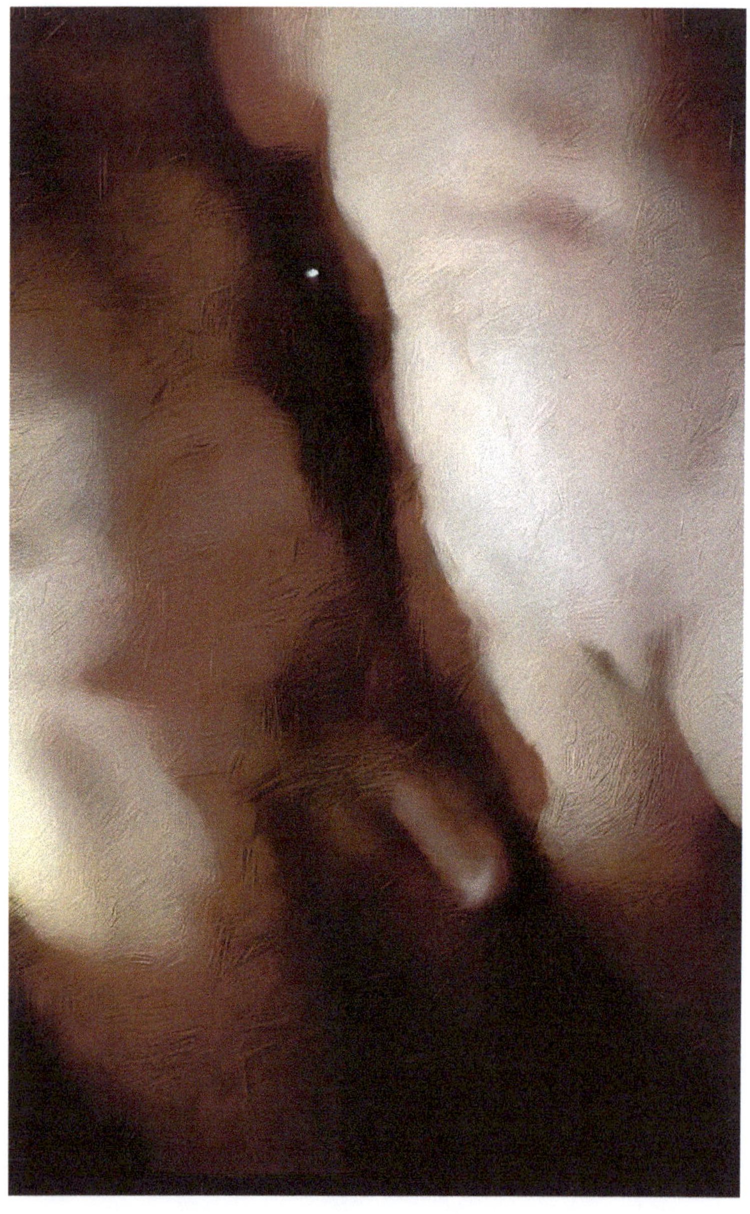

Xiaoqiu Qiu

Lime around Seine

I've only now noticed it was charged
in euros, my Lime pass, and that in the front basket
the empty bag of ficelle and an azure umbrella,
makes my heart fall out when
I see someone's poem about
past is irretrievably present,

> Noon tides up the plane tree shadows
> drop them soft sprinkles of gravels
> rise, I go up, up, washing my face in
> and out their freckled silence, the bikes, the strollers,
> the light denim pants, in and out, the shades, and in
> the Eiffels back and forth in the hands of peddlers,
> the chevalier's fingers gilded over onto the next
> each entangles a lateness a second ago

—simply, *j'arrive*
the time that is a place when in third grade
Wednesday afternoon school ends early at 3,
teachers gather us at the hall, portraits of Gorky and Mao,
it could have been, "*depechez-vous, les enfants!*"
I'm blanking on the exact words,
and we start to paddle, home is over a bridge
Au-Bau never takes down his earbuds,
Yan-Yan has a loud sneeze
and chinese plane trees, *vuton*, have leaves shape of our palms
their shadows spindly brush past our cheeks:

dark, light, dark, light
in the paddle, paddle, paddle, conducting our singing:

> *"Cet air qui m'obsède jour et nuit*
> *Cet air n'est pas né d'aujourd'hui*
> *Il vient d'aussi loin que je viens*
> *Traîné par cent mille musiciens"*

I saw Au-Bau just now in the crowd, in front of stoplight on cours-la-reine—
I had seen him in Shanghai, 29th floor, but I couldn't see him, his
white shirt and black tie—*mais si, c'est lui!* I know those eyes!
That one, next to the police car, blue scooter, black dress, AirPods, bra
showing a little, the way she folds her neck so slightly over shoulder
the afternoon cloud leans on another, forgets to move
the wind, the music, the eyes,
the city
they're not born here today, they come as far as I have come.

> the Airbnb host teaches at Sorbonne, and has a bookshelf of Emil
> Cioran, in new and dusted, "Being born was a catastrophe," he says,
> "a fact survivors try to flee from". and the Seine under Eiffel
> continues
> to smell like pisspots and fish scales when I walk towards it, and the
> sun continues
> to knead gold waves behind me when I walk past it, in secret, as the
> past second
> had just exiled this one, as birth has exiled us when we were born,
> as we turn, for a home,
> and catch some shards of halos in our iris, and turn back,
> wonder which darkened stair we had just descended from, bleedin

Raymond Rosales

River Morel

Sugar Water Lilies

Prowess of you; steaming boning moan
of you, I call tonight. Will our hands become
sugar water, ever again? As when I suck
on your fingers & you drive? Will you catch
fire and me, me, pulsate electricity?
I miss feeling the true earth of green under my feet.
I have greater wishes than your thrones. These garage
hands love it. I mean, getting huddled down through
moans, I mean, calling florists over butchered boxes
of water lilies
Your eyes like frozen puddles, or black magnets
Boring into me, spitting your heart out at me, causing
me to groan
Never think back on what could be true. Personally,
I found the real answer through bargaining. The reason
I loved you was unclear. Or do I just regard it, as a dream,
ghost of a feeling?
Stem of plant unfounding. Iterations of the mood will
cause a rupture in the blank. In sorrow, in gold, in
holy matrimony. I'm slowly uncurling my esophagus
from my bodice, and hand-passing it out my mouth.
So worship these playing lines
These strings which cause rich music --
They have ends approaching, too

James Cariddi

The Internet

In those heady, first few years after Al Gore helped
develop across our great nation the infrastructure of
an information superhighway, hope abounded.
The Hopi of northern Arizona, in fact, whose traditions
have survived into the internet age
because upon encountering
conquistadores for the first time in 1540 they resolved
to test
the would-be-divinity of those visitors seeming to be
envoys of Quetzalcoatl
and finding their ability to fulfill prophecy wanting
in spite of their bearded appearance and easterly
arrival
expelled them from their pueblos before they could
establish a foothold
believed at the dawn of the millennium so strongly
in the transformative power of technology to transcend
our earthly forms in favor of the great eternal truth
that the final panel of a six-part mural painted at the time
by two tribal artists depicts their history as culminating
in a computer sitting atop the Pyramid of the Serpent from
Teotihuacan surrounded by symbols from religions around
the world.
That mural, Hopi Visions: Journey of the Human Spirit,
was packed up and sent to Dallas during the Trump
administration. But, back in the time of Panel Five,
around 1999, just before the demarcation
after which people generally readily googled

anything they didn't know,
While the Hopi struggled against the ravaging effects of fast
food, pollution, and crushing poverty
I was learning about the crucifixion in CCD class.
Our teacher told us about how Christ, nailed to the cross,
was offered vinegar, or according to some sources sour wine,
through a sponge affixed to a reed by a Roman soldier.
From the context, it wasn't clear to us if this was a minor mercy
or yet another mockery, and Mr. Jasko didn't know either.
Later,
Mr. Gore told us hurricanes would get worse and after the laughter we
still called them Sandy, Irma and Maria instead of Cincinatus or Randy
Travis, despite his "I Told You So" hitting number one the same
year a starry-eyed Al, later reported to have then believed Love Story
was based on his own life, first made a run for president
Distracted as we've been.
But anyway, as it turned out, the Roman soldier, named
Stephaton, most likely meant no harm when he offered
that so-called vinegar, as a more accurate translation
would have linked the drink with posca, a refreshing
concoction of coriander, salt and other spices infused into
a diluted vinegar as a sort of ancient gatorade. He'd have
probably gave Jesus a like if he could—perhaps even shared
the sorry scene from his personal feed.

"visitors seeming to be envoys of Quetzalcoatl"

Karin Falcone Krieger

Plastic Fruit Sutra

Fake fruit basket
        a still life of lies
                a Mid-century why?
Faithful reproduction
        devoid of nutrition
                down to the spots on the banana.
Bananas are perfect
        phony phones
                Ernie and Bert say   Hello?
                                Hello?

Grapes semi-translucent
                green or mauve, soft
                        Pluck one off
        sharp brown tooth of plastic stem
a bland bite, dry
        Climb to sink
                fill with water
                        an April Fool surprise!
What could be said
        of the apple, pear and orange
                except the sound of
                        when they roll
                                across the linoleum
                                        basket upset
                                                by its own static sorry.

"Dreams can only prophesy the most mundane things."
– Anthony Burgess

Man on the wanted poster is your lover. You have just brought him to Christmas dinner and everyone loved him. You are about to get on the train to leave and see the poster of him there. Criminal.

Institutionalized. Sky white as a piece of paper. From beach to beach they close down the strips too late and a tarantula wakes whirlpools in the sand. Turtle has no shell and licks away at fish food.

You have two bats - pipes. But you think they are whistles - flutes. You finally realize they are bird calls. The cardinal and the mourning dove wake us from sleep.

Nights of HBO: California cops canyons country sides: thinks of work vs. school, family vs. alone and a prospect of romance: each the substitute for the other as it stands.

There's the ditch and there's the water you want the latter, dressed in grey underwear. Surrogate danger in dormant clothes.

Add dresses.

Creeley said, "…for bad Italian and twisted bridges…"

In one reality you read only the introductions to books. That is all you need to know. In one reality you are a lean dancer, in another you are a fat dancer, in another you are no dancer at all - a watcher. It is not about politics: it is literature. So choose.

Green Grows Wild in His World

It agrees with him, means go, greets him
       when he boots up. Green
           is his high tech and rustic
               green is his mansmell and distant
          all the things that make him say
      what's your favorite color
It's political; it's primordial
           and it is working, working for him
             at his speed
             its his karma. Green
         can't catch up to verdigris
      but can choke out open space.
Irish Spring and a pocket knife green
       Fucking on pine needles green
          "It's not easy being green."
              The frog who moves with ease
      from water to land and to jump into the air
Let's take the frog to be our
         mascot for green:
      moving through the elemental
daring to slip through all occasions.

Green eyes and bottle flies.
       Weeds up from cracks now
         Corroded battery patina green
       Green eggs and grouches

Weekend warrior stalking the wild____________
         has paid the highest price
            There in his pocket is where the arrowroot
      exuberance exhausts itself.

       Clearly this is a winner!
         A remarkable absinthe!
       A romance of next thing!
A manly kind of plant like ivy:
       it just grows, pinnate and foliate
            one leaf at a time.
       I've got Fibonacci's number...
a new leaf every day.

Sight of Blood

No relief from the ache in my teeth. I yearned to sink them into living meat. PBS *Nature* offers a snow leopard. "She and other great cats go for the jugular, drink the blood of the stunned animal…" Ibex staggers and sways. The sharp toothed mammal returns for more drink.

I wished the swollen sun would send a torrent of blood and stunned pigeons. It would be as rain was once. I dream a greyish snowfall that leaves black puddles of cool blood.

"The great cats must clamp necks of large prey for as long as an hour to kill them. Not like hyenas, jackals, or wild dogs that eat their prey alive by going for the scruff or the belly." They hang on until the pack arrives to feast on the guts of wildebeest, digested grass perhaps also one unborn.

The many foods not eaten in the refrigerator are monuments that one day an appetite will return for rice as well as rain. Rare steak in a restaurant as a show of faith just left me for a sickness.

Over the bar the news says a doctor fell asleep on his feet with a beating human heart in his hand. She died. A central wound better not be red. A glass of red

"I pierced my tongue not because I was afraid of needles, not because I was unwilling to speak…" I saw the snow leopard tattooed on his shin. That made it very easy to talk to him.

B. A. Kocsis

Empire of Innocence No.1

Musik

Domestic Sheol

Meat that is more wheat and sorghum than meat
Fruit that is not real fruit
Fruit made of water
Eco dish cleaner and spray
Cheap paper towel to clean up after cooking
A life without life

Venus! Give me back my Demons!

I want Fire
Merkaba
      Celestial chariots
         Of blue, and green

And, now
On a weekday

Wednesday

You fall asleep with me reading to you

And I stare
With
My visions on the ceiling

Two cream legs cut off at the abdomen on a blue sheet

You look down at them
full of tenderness that negated sense
"I have missed you," you smile, admire
the cute freckles on their nose and the tops of their shoulders
dimples of their smile and the tooth,
slightly bigger than the rest, that they had 'fixed'
in Chile.
Their arms, a little chubby, kissable, that drape over your neck and
                                          draw

              you

    in

"I've missed our game," they reply.
You look up to see a victory grin, as if they made a bad pun.

While cleaning up
they ask
"Is it true people feel bad after sex?"
"Sometimes." You say, "The French call it the little death,
la petite mort"

"*La Grande Mort*" They say,
dying
throwing themselves back, half-
                    hanging over the edge of the bed.

"I'll go start dinner."

Not Jealous

Drink cinnamon whiskey in Finland.
Remember my sister,
in Australia, writing her poetry
which is better than mine.

Cameron Charles Martin

Some Ogre

Pause a look on the fête with the faintest of ire before a clamber toward the kitchen, untoward a harry of the margaret at the hob, short reëntrant with a gob of roux, stood like the rook from some romance, with a hand on the beam in a kind of threat. And then he lurches on a boulder's path driven long the marches of the civilized, and oil poised to drop from his mustaches, eyeing wrothly the lamps, the salver, treading a spiral and softening; soft with mint and gummed with treacle, he and his sprig set upon her, his thumb spread on his sleeve, a stave to print upon her cheek as candles saunter past and cast they two in trembles on the wall while the smalls of the goblets make vapors and by twos time divides itself.

Suddenly I start accumulating. Rows of red stones in a cave and a pile of marrow.

I think of nothing else.

Bottomless Autumn, Full of Sun

Got done with not feeling well people need to listen to me
this glut of children, even three percent will be too many puppeteers
how can you insist on any grade of man's desiderata
here I lie, withdrawing consent like a foehn, fresh heat
and punctual, discrete confusion see them bobbing in canals like rats
at midnight I will laugh my head off a laugh like ice in craquelure
it can be simple if I insist
it'll be tidied up for whoever arrives remember I was thinking of you
I saw the color of the ribbons in a dream jets of living slush with slush-
faces
a girl in line with a choker on binding her together, buying tablets
people lurch like homunculi
and I too am sulking in the loggia
it can't be right, first the wind licks you
then the clouds part and there's the sun big smug face of an assailant
if I had a cape it would be rich and pale uncted with a haze of sweet
tailings
and thick like daylight couldn't impregnate but if you started to stagger
out would come my hand a gift, a designation
something like an attar, imagine tomorrow might be full of cowards a
caste of faces incubating
neither me nor me

Willy Conley

Everglades John Boats II

Michael Starr

Civilized dinosaurs society

Say what they men
Men them self
Wise, dinosaur
Wise,
Sendt-033
Wrong hat
Dinosaur
Went on spree
For fresh depths
For canine lemurs
For a spin out the
Spin
Dinosaur, why
You leap
Straddle the mark
Head West
Head West

Adele Nwankwo

ya jah gah hah

"navigating a white male world was not threatening. it wasn't even interesting. i was more interesting than they were. i knew more than they did. and i wasn't afraid to show it."
— toni morrison

flit crit stit writ me in to mist tick
hinge match want give me his white dick say no mist ta he say no give
give
like am queen o' tha car rib yin speak in pidgin ya speak real idgit
voodoo prak tik casta oyal drip drip no get i like shakes peeya (*o tel lo?*)
chagal bas kee aht duh vor ich
be law w*man gol watch wrist wrist only want wife go mast a mast a
yis
yis flit crit stit writ dis bitch in to mist tick soon fine out me make fresh
blooms go fist fis

After Coming Out: A Wrestling Promo

If I were a wrestler – one of those real juicy, full-of-trenbalone, moonsault-off-the-top, meathead beefcake types, my coming out might've gone a little differently. I would've been intimidating; wouldn't have tripped up on so many of my necessary words. But now, all I can do is try to save face, like:

> *Thanks, Mean Gene. You wanna know know I feel today?*
> *You wanna know how I <u>feel</u> after being cheated out of a victory over Pat*
> *Patriarchy at Survivor Series? I'm furious. I'm <u>hot</u>. Ooh, I'm so mad I could kiss*
> *a woman I don't even like right now!*
> *Yeah, I see all you pretty ladies in the crowd right there. Ric Flair might be*
> *broken-down old Magic Mountain, but I'm Raging Bull at Six F(l)ags. Step*
> *right up!* (Gotta give them something to cheer for, right?)

And then Mean Gene would've cut in to keep me on track and probably would've pointed out the bandages above my eyes, on my arms, and heart, before asking,
What's the move now? Aren't
you too banged up to wrestle? Maybe you should do what most do when a coming
out doesn't go their way and buy a pint of B n' J's ice cream and eat your feelings.

> To which I would have replied:
> *You see these cuts? You see these bruises?*
> *These are nothin'! Nothin'!! I'm just wearin' this shit 'cause the therapist*
> *wouldn't let me leave their office without 'em.*
> ** tears off copious amounts of gauze wrapping and cotton* AAAH! You see*
> *that? The CisBoys thought they could gang up on me and put an end to my*
> *championship title pursuit? Hah!*
> *I've got Toni Morrison books that hit harder than those bozos. When I get my*
> *hands on 'em, they'll get what's comin' to 'em.*

Oh, and this would've lit the crowd ablaze, caused them
to whisk and rattle their homemade signs ("The Nigerian Nightmare,"
"Nwankwo 11:16," "Step on My Balls, Kween Adele!")
And then Mean Gene, catching the producer's wrap-up signal,
would have proffered a few final queries: *Where do you go from here?*

*Who do you wanna face tonight? Do you think you can convince the world to accept
you as champion?*

And I would have said: *You'd better believe ol' PP's gettin' a Spectrumifier
(that'd be my finisher) reeeeal soon. But before I get to him and the CisBoys,
I've got
a few loose ends to tie up, startin' with Best Friend Friedman, who sold me out
last week in my time of need. Then it's the Family Alliance, for not havin' my
back when I was getting jumped and for blaming me
for it backstage afterward in their promo. But Gene, can I convince the world?
You see these 7" pythons?
You see this 38" waist? There's not a person alive who can stop me.
And they're just gonna have to accept me for what and <u>who</u> I am.*

That's when I'd brusquely brush past MG and storm out of the shot to
deafening adulation, a crafty rival lying in wait,
and a long, difficult journey to the Idpol Intercontinental
Championship.

At least, that's how I imagine the aftermath of my coming out would
have gone—in a different life, perhaps.
(I was the one eating ice cream on the couch

Ken Edward Rutkowski

Singing Poet

I want to be a singing poet see by song by wind I go by two heads and all I can find is this dream from within now the poet sings on this Earth like cleaning his Bell across the sky with birds written down nothing found but I wanna be singing High-C up in the sun I want to be nothing but High He just for fun see the poet it's not me I haven't seen them both at the same time you must sign the fallacy to stay above the line connect the prophecy of living free want to be a singing poet I believe that we'll find we're broken like bones and teeth I grind into the feet the soil is ground and prime from all the bugs tilling around with their toes and nails you end up doing that all the time both boats towards the same sun to the end of the world go far into Infinity so I may breathe the song let's sing along I need the signs to follow my runs solid seeds I want to be walking free countries beings going through mirrors blind two heads three souls 3 nudes in the buff in the water in the pool in the summer time you see rays come down and bless us one by one to be one will come free come see you understand I don't wanna undo being a man why is it too little too late am I mad what am I they ask me don't ask me they asked me what I wanted to be when I was young I never knew and I don't know now you understand not supposed to I know no longer the man I want to be a singing poet C when I was a pharaoh breathing inside the egg through the shell I was told what I already knew an almond beginning all along inside my shell singing now in the sun in the wind it's all been from within the sun goes up and down in the rain in the cold until the waves come in saying San Diego to the shells to the granules of sound that mip mip I hear the singing I hear the ringing I hear the sound boggling in my mind I'm homeless now poet psalm power the wrong pitch no one believes me I'm breathing in Polish I know to the wind the problem echoing itself away we have 3 little sweet undeserved rhymes for the defenseless children who hold hands may hold hands the prophecy the solitary mind in the sky as sung now in dormancy two months 2 heads 2 New Years sitting in a chair by a table eating that stuff that ain't mine for they don't phone ya if they don't know ya when I was little I was little but I was already singing 'he say God' I don't say God don't help him help me.

Golden Bear

ground down by body worn bake side sun ahead of him like a drama into his eyes into his black mind arrows through each one inside two ears the bear walks along now found in main red sun Half Dome on top of his head brings an old hat when he goes to the moon rocks older box on the ground big boulders he pushed aside with his hands in between narrow alleys of red blood down inside the eyes of Big Bear closed through Old Town ascends mountains beside sons of Catholic worship into big temple line Bear Bear there's something there I don't see him anywhere looking back smiles pulls up inside sphere the top goes in half and half of the sun all primary colors the same dance on minimum anyway of Martiano it all gotta go like Mary Mumbles to herself on with all things that overthink themselves himself XYZ DD Davis summer in Lebanon number over there was my love Cortana model woman spits on the ground spits on the ground one other thing even the banging around known about him some say some ball it's all about momentum Sony Sony on high! he said in the main corner in the bell here in there the sun gallons I never asked about it they come back in you know invented all the gardens on the server I need things I've done it comes down to bare gums only tell Tina Sam well the number one honey nothing left in varying there among the noise in the song into his head on into his minor black arrow decline not nothing but arrows cropped up in space in the bar he holds up the sun Half Dome it comes off his head tilts it like the world is a better dance on insane it's almost that it comments on who you are big Batman scene and then it's Alice teen Internet Shelly barrel on bar in the bars in the hiring in Lawrence and any posting thing on backing by backing down there Dallas both at night light no longer known under golden yellow download where is Apples is she back in the ground background rocks all black space now without sight.

The Weatherman

Where did all the women go hauling their carts up the street in the sun selling avocados mangoes sour apples the ladies who made com tam every day from 6 to 1 now gone the man who used to fix my shoes polish them brown mend the laces for free had a stack of shoes so high he could not see me the fruit lady in the market with the gray tabby cat swatting people's shoes the food sui cao banh xeo bun ca bun rieu bahn mi goi cuon nem nuong where did it all go the Americans French Vietnamese South Africans Brits Russians the Koreans Dutch and Chinese where did they all go the security guards the lifeguards the fisherman the whole collective of Tan Dinh all the families that sold most of the food the children the people in the park with their roller skates on all wearing their masks just like you asked walking the loop smashing balls with their feet under trees the immaculate flowers in rows the motorbikes the noise the traffic where did it all go and their names My Hang I almost forgot her name she sold me coffee and gave me snacks put my art up on her wall the only frame with a picture inside and Huong who swept our alley every day I gave him one of my shirts he fixed the mirror on my bike do you know their names or when they might be back it rains every day the sun still shines my worst fear is that I stop saying hello hi how are you what is your name invisible clouds blocking out our view of the sun I have never seen the Weatherman have you but I would ask him what are their names and what will you say when you look up at the sky and that big mirror ball is gone what will you do will they recognize you will they even know your name?

Robert Esposito

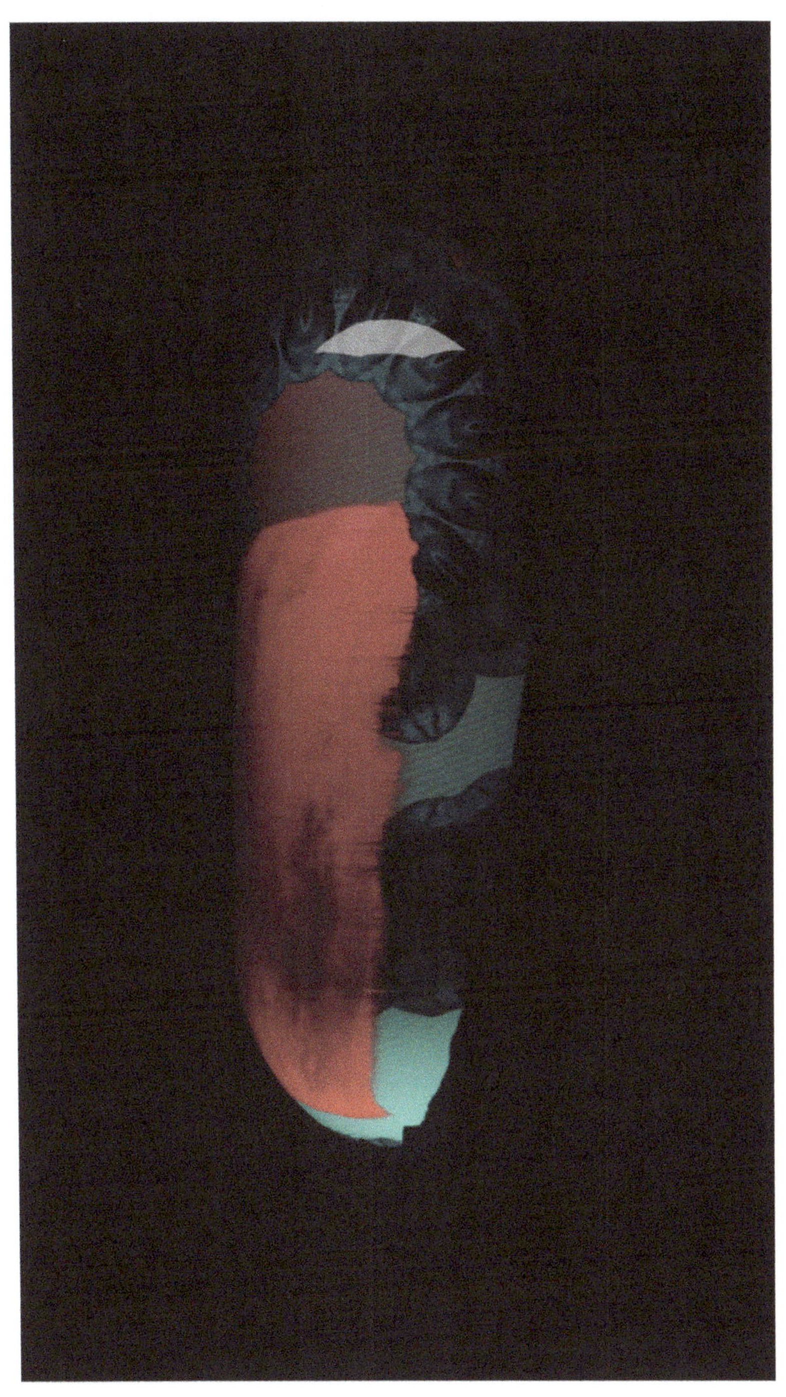

Lucie Chou

Sabrina as a Hot Spring in Mashyuza, Rwanda

I dreamt that my legs were covered with plants growing out of my skin. What does this dream mean?

The smallest wayerlily in the world, Nymphaea thermarum, was discovered by Eberhard Fischer in 1987, who, seeing their last extant habitat so vulnerable, sent live specimens to Bonn Botanic Gardens. As Rwandan farmers diverted the hot spring on which the waterlilies were dependent to irrigate fields and supply a local laundry, the species went extinct in the wild. One of the ones preserved in Bonn was eaten by a rat, and another was stolen. As Nymphaea teetered on the brink of total extinction, Carlos Magdalena at Kew induced seeds to germinate and grow to maturity successfully. He wrote on an article that one day the resuscitated "pygmy Rwandan waterlily" might make its way around the world as a popular houseplant.

I fell feet-first into a mesh of little rills running over fine iridescent silt. My flesh tingled with glints of tactile titters. Sweet, silent, I sat then lay down in the lukewarm water, feeling buried shallowly in the sand earth's hot shivering heart.

Ah the immersion! Emollient, medicinal, my oneiric muse

The next thing I lay firmly yet fluently embedded in the sabulous skin, my limbs transsubstantiated into limpid lymph. I am Sabrina, rising from Limbo. I am a reticulum of tiny rivers, my flesh and blood indistinguishable, my consanguinity with this warm pocket of earth perfect. I am a blooming nymph, my arms and legs nursing grounds of Nymphaea. I nourish these small lilies with my smooth luscious body burning with love.

Glossy green spangles gathered at the root grow in rosettes

Veined villous sepals glabrous pale petals golden genitals

Born early morning die just a little
after noon

Second morning your other half's second coming

Temporal divide
of your hermaphrodite floral functionings

Protogynous
large seeds, few tubers tropic day bloomer

My gaiety is your gladness, my health your bounty, my pygmy renascent beauties.
Mother Goddess, Great Earth, this succubous solid thing, whose spirit I am, slowly
over-stirring, I am Her nymph.
You last five sisters, my nymphs, my nymphaea, I am your nymphaeum. Your
lifeblood. Rare radiant maidens, you are rooted in me.
But I lived only in that dream. When I awoke, it was into death. Your death, because
mine. When my dream fled, it was flushed into fouled fabrics, frothing in farmers'
fields of famine. My body a distempered, drouthy nothing. All that remained of my
soul was the bleary memory of a man whose hands hewed two small hollows in my
shriveling flesh, held two uprooted nymphs then hospiced them in foreign lands.
Briefly the two of you bloomed and bore seed, before one became food in a rat's
belly, the other gold in a thief's wallet. All that remained of the memory was that after
thousands of thwarted trials, eight seeds sprouted in a greenhouse, where another
man hailing to the legendary name of Plant Messiah tried to reunite my soul and body.
Water and Earth, in perfect proportion and constitution, one at the exact same level
with the other, not one inch of drouth or drowning. My thermal homeostasis, 25
degrees Celsius. All that your roots remembered was to suckle the skin of what they
knew as mother. They flourished again, found the lost dream. It was my spectre,
summoned by Messiah Magdalena. Was it to be your salvation?

Extinct in the wild horticultural gospel on windowsill

Self-Portrait with 300 Houseplants

Could plants ever evolve enough to become sentient?

These quarantine days the rosy-fingered stonecrops ogle like household gods about to swoop down on me. I picture Leda levitating in the invisible vises of a giant bird of paradise which is really a pair of *Monstera deliciosa* leaves. In hours before dawn, in the dim window recess, my five pots of squash vine in sweet repose are savannahs of elephants sleeping with their ears shielding one another's bodies. A golden glare makes the glass disappear & a blossom opens its hirsute beak like a prehistoric bee. My hybrid orchids have gone haywire or hyperpathic. I fumble to their perches to find lucid opal eyes of apsaras fluttering out at my reposeless lids as butterflies with as many as nine pairs of wings each.

What are your golden stigmata my goddesses stars or sacred scars
If plants are gods, they filter splendor of the sun into my mind as the vision that they are made by parent divinities who, divining the efficacy of venomous thorns and plasticophagous haustoria, implanted those things in plants, while being themselves, vegetal beings, their own and everything's beginning. Plants invented themselves and their myths; after that, they initiated noetic innovations: ideas of biological coevolution; symbiosis; biophilia. Implanted those beliefs; instilled Amortentia in me. Even gods long for mortal affection in their lonely moments. I am comforted by the conviction that my damask roses, blooming a ghastly ashen white all through winter, are lovesick for a little caress, creature comfort, maybe a human embrace.

> On my balcony
> she breathes a sigh, masturbates then
> sweetens my tea

In my newfound silence, plants talk back to me. I stand before their soil-stained paper tags as if awaiting oracles: Paper Pinwheel, Blush Pink, Salmon Peach, Yellow Paw, Cream Puff. Oxalis, put my eyes out with your popping seeds. With my hair dripping, I open my window to the deserted street. Sleety gusts slap my face like ghosts of cold concrete. I hear a voice calling me the hyacinth girl. No. Here am I, nursing these hyacinth nymphs serried on my windowsill. On the brink of spring, ephemeral & effervescent adolescents all. I call back, one by one: Anna Marie, Pink Pearl, White Pearl, Innocence, Blue Star, Delft Blue, Lady Derby, Fondante, Amethyst, Gypsy Queen, Red Rocket, Rose of Naples, Dreadnought. Under whose incipient inflorescence I find a chrysalis.

> O pupa, darling
> girl, doll, in your dream goldshell world in a
> wildflower

If someone asks if they should ever evolve into sentient creatures, behold them dancing with me in my jungle chamber. By turns I wear fiddle-leaf fig trees, Swiss cheese plants and baby saguaros on my shoulder like Kylie Jenner sporting the faux lion head. It has been said that it stands for the wildness within the creative soul. The creative soul that

> springs off my naked clavicle to
> cleave floorboards with viriditas

Voices from Under the Forest Floor

Listen. We have withdrawn underground. Into brown roots.
We have pruned time back. We have undone what you did to us.
Returned to before mutilation.

We have shorn our long lashing bodies of trauma. Here in the
chthonic, where scimitars' cutthroat
curves can no more gash us, we stridulate our safely folded fronds like
sleeping cicadas.
We refuse to give our skin to be peeled, unplaited, sopped, reduced to
paper pulp.
Don't call us curtailed by cruelty. Call us returned to our roots.
The root of *passion*
is to *suffer, endure.* We return to our roots to hiss great passion from
underground labyrinths.
We have retired into the invisible. We live on. Just will not go on
living for you.
Don't call us dead. Call us hibernating in your moral fimbulwinter.
We glitter darkly like unlit veins of gold. We are visifugal like magic
necklaces of buds. We are sinuous, sinewy vegetal lodes. We scuff our
coarse skin on cool soil.
We are sly as ropey bones concealed in the silky paste of a sponge
cake. Dig your hungry sawtooth blades into our brown dense matrix.
Feel how we hurt. We can feel fertilizer filtering into the finely filled
fissures between one of us and another.
Feed us the burnt bone dust of scribomanic fingers. Sprinkle it
generously on the surface over us, a sacrificial frost. Spade it in. Let us
feel it fermenting on our skin.
Rain will swill down, maelstrom the bonemeal into manna-milk.
We will drink death like divine justice.

Allie Cabal

Enviable

"We are sly as ropey bones concealed in the silky paste"

Addy Gravatte

Suggestive

"Once they had protected his senseless everywhere..."

Bodywork (2 pages)

2-

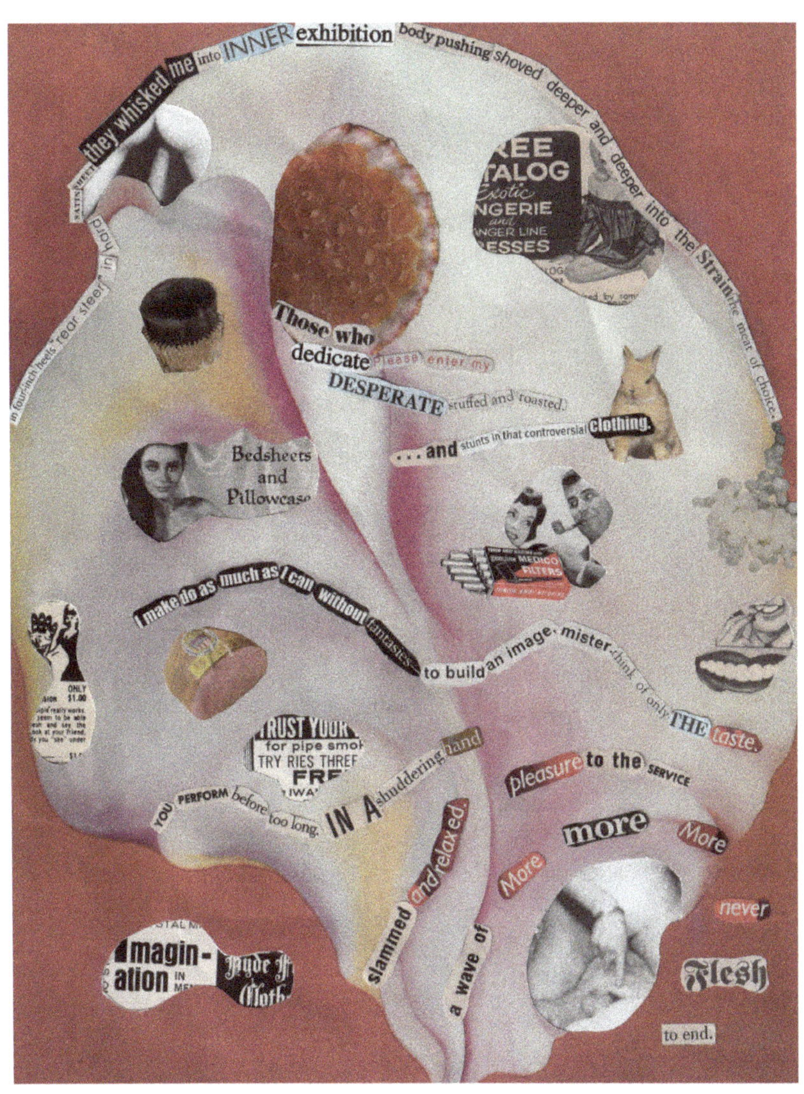

they whisked me into INNER exhibition body pushing shoved deeper and deeper into the Strainine meat of choice.
Those who dedicate please enter my DESPERATE stuffed and roasted.
...and stunts in that controversial clothing.
Bedsheets and Pillowcase
I make do as much as I can without fantasies to build an image, mister-chunk of only THE taste.
pleasure to the SERVICE
YOU PERFORM before too long. IN A shuddering hand
slammed and relaxed
a wave of
more More More
never
to end.
Flesh
imagin-ation
MEDICO FILTERS
ONLY $1.00

Peyton Fultz

Nathair acrylic on canvas, 2022

Grant McGrath

Evanesce

My Body

Debbra Palmer

Chewed Up

I was well into my 30s before I realized that I could, if I wanted to, chew an entire pack of gum one piece after another. As a kid, we rationed our gum and candy. Sometimes, we even saved it after we'd licked, chewed, or sucked on it for a while.

Highlighter Lord

Whenever someone refers to the "blue-eyed, blonde" Jesus I always think of a feminine figure. The cartoonish presentation filled in with highlighter colors resulted in a crude stained-glass effect. Drawing and painting Christ in these bright colors with eyeshadow and lips felt irreverent at first, but then I saw him as someone I might actually want to talk to.

At the Feet of the Replica of the Christus, Utah

Among the airbrushed kingdoms of glory
it looks as if you could buy a shaved ice.
It's not where you'd expect to see Christ

or his big toe and his pinkie toe and the rest
of his toes like piglets, sound asleep,
having suckled their mother clean.

Here, Jesus has toes like Vienna sausages
in a baby food jar, ten small toes his mother
counted and kissed and pretended to eat.

Here is the big toe he stubbed on the temple steps
before saying, *God damn it to hell.*
Shoe salesmen weep here, as do whores.

Hell, there's even a hymn about it-- *'till we meet,*
'till we meet, 'till we meet at Jesus's feet.
Bring your oil, bring your tears. Bring long hair.

The panorama of a three-story kingdom
our brethren built with stolen plans reserves the bottom floor
for people like me. In the celestial penthouse,

they serve ambrosia for breakfast, middle level,
eggs Florentine. My people eat from vending machines
in a basement with no windows.

Jesus, I pray to these marble copies of your feet,
Why did you give them the keys to our house?
They say I will never see you again.

I thought that if I could pray as a boy I would feel

something that girls cannot. And I wanted to feel it.
I tried it as if kneeling with my father,
and I was his good and faithful boy. I imagined him saying, *son,
victories are won while you are on your knees.* And as I prayed,
the Holy Spirit would fill us both from crown to chest until we glowed,
then, yes! split us from heart to groin. We would weep,
ugly, open throated and *sore* afraid.
The first light would come, an angel, holding a white-hot coal
to our lips. Undone, we would open our eyes.

But it was nothing like this.

Instead, I was a girl who prayed the way a seed prays
to a crack in the sidewalk: *If you don't mind,*

that is, if you don't mind.

Silvia Perry

2
JOY
IS A FORM OF
RESISTANCE

Anne Pedone

Untitled: From The Goethe Institute

It was only that I was on the subway
this morning reading about how
some guys in
Rome were out drinking when one of them found
the head from an
ancient status of
Venus
And now everyone in Rome fucks like an American.
Since I was seven I've never slept alone.

"And now everyone in Rome fucks like an American"

Aleksandra Scepanovic

Hinge of Selves

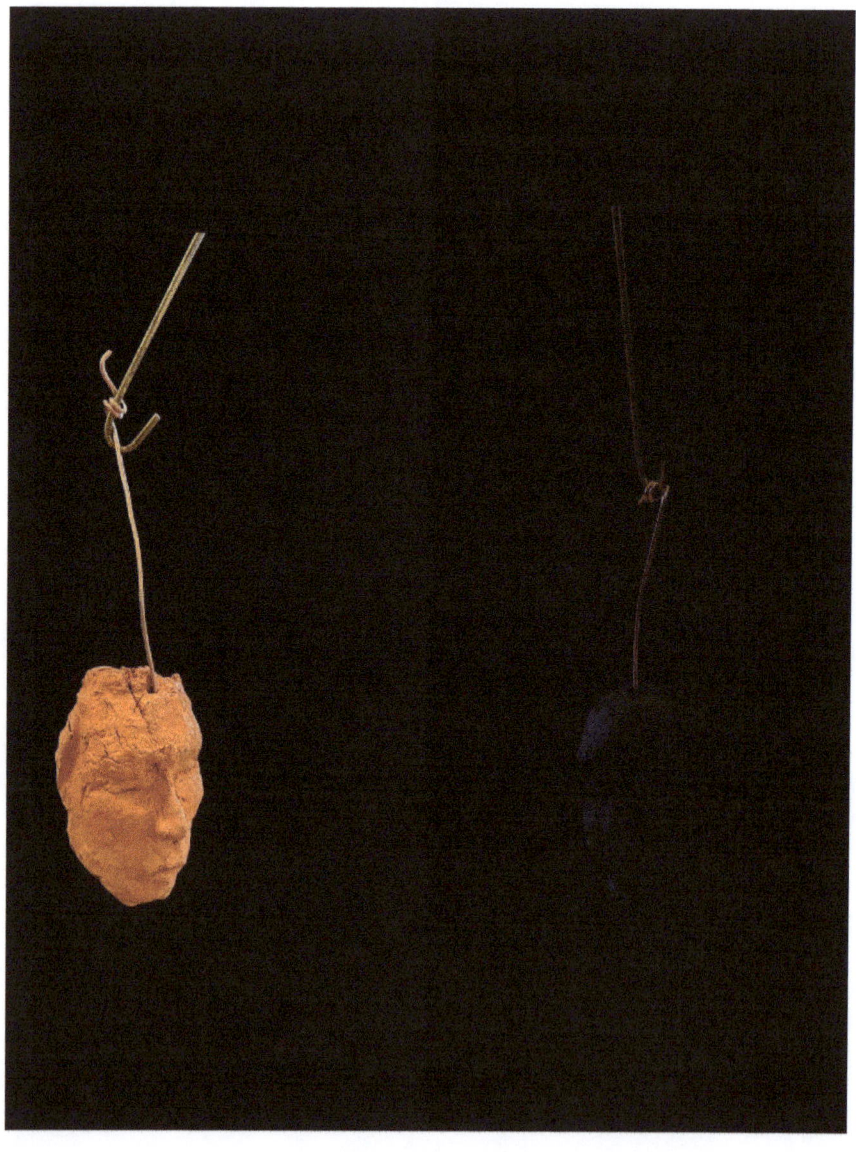

La Vieillesse

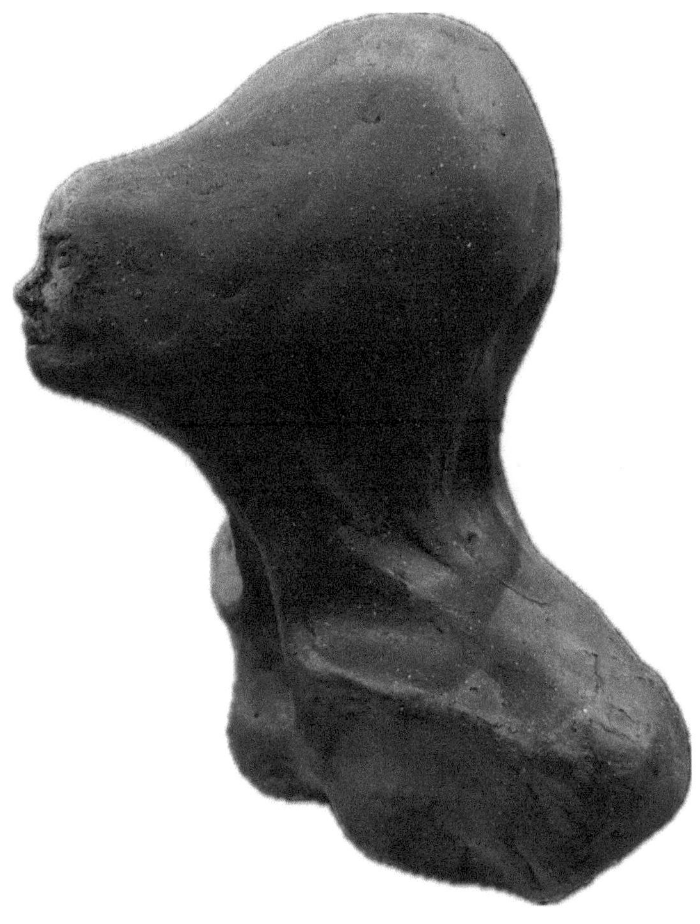

Nik Orlando

Komorebi 1

Feeling Nirvana

CONTRIBUTORS

Jay Aelick The gray catbird's second-biggest fan. X of Wands incarnate. Mouth of Truth survivor. 1/2 of the Saint Balasar University English Club podcast.

Abol Bahadori My mom told me that I started scribbling before I started talking. I believe that is why painting is my primary method of expression. I was born in Tabriz, the capital city of Iranian Azerbaijan. Tabriz is the city of carpets and miniatures. As a child, I was inspired by colorful abstract motifs on rugs. I started painting at a very early age and won the "Best Young Artist" prize at age nine among the local schools. I moved to France and England during my youth. I earned a bachelor's degree in Fine Arts and Textile Design and a master's degree in Digital Application Design from the University of Manchester, UK, before settling in the DC area, where I took training from the founders and followers of Washington Color School starting in the '90s. I have worked in various creative fields throughout my career. As a fabric designer, graphic designer, art director, and currently a full-time artist at the Torpedo Factory Art Center (Studio 5), I have relied solely on the fine arts and my continuous painting process as a solid foundation for creative development. Painting is my livelihood, as well as a foundation for my professional life. I consider myself more of a colorist. For me, color is everything. Color comes before shape and form. It creates space, dimension, and—most importantly—feelings. We humans view the world through a limited spectrum. But what if we had compound eyes like insects, sonar like dolphins, or even used scent to perceive our surroundings? I'm drawn to the space between the known and the unknown. Art is a doorway to the subconscious, and color opens the path. My artistic process is a journey through the colors that occur to my eyes, as composers would hear the notes in their ears. The process is spontaneous. It happens outside of the realm of self and intellect. Forms come in to represent the colors. More than an artist, I consider myself a medium to provide the observer (including myself) access to the unknown or the forgotten. My art is successful only when viewers see their story in it and connect to the self and the universe through it. Listening to what others see in my paintings, I am continually surprised by our shared collective memory.

J'han Brady Born in San Jose, California (1982) and currently living in Washington, D.C. / Baltimore, MD region, J'han is an emerging contemporary artist who is driven by her creativity, informed by her curiosity, and inspired by her experiences, and works within sculpture, drawing, painting, and installation art, with a recognizably unique style best described as experimental.

Stephen Brown (he/him) is a writer-activist with a Philly attitude and a background in LGBT+ Studies. Managing Editor of *Rathalla Review* and graduate student completing his MFA at Rosemont College, Stephen's fiction and poetry have appeared in *SCAB Mag, Beneath the Soil, Querencia Press, Wicked Gay Ways*, and others.

Charlie Becker is a retired speech pathologist who now studies and writes poetry with the Community Literature Initiative in Los Angeles. He also has helped bring poetry to under-served high school students through the Living Writers Series and L.A. Unified School District. Charlie's first book of poetry and drawings, Friends My Poems Gave Me, was published by World Stage Press in 2016. He has also had poems published by Passager Journal, Comstock Review, The Dandelion Review, and Silver Pinion. Charlie lives with his partner, Aubry, in Laguna Woods, California.

Gordon Blitz at as a child was called a sissy, girlie, fag, queer, and homo. Getting towel whipped, stomach punched and spit on were part of his world. His father, who died after Gordon's Bar Mitzvah, berated him with shouts of "Walk straight." Gordon never found his writer's voice until he retired in 2017 from forty years of accounting and became a passionate writing machine. During 2020, Gordon had published work in Whoa Nelly Press, Wingless Dreamer, Two Hawks Quarterly, the Santa Monica College Journals Chronicles and On Going Moments, and Gay Wicked Ways. In 2021 his best- selling novel "Shipped Off" was published and is also available as an audiobook. On February 2022, his second novel "Fathers and Other Strangers" was published. He will soon publish his gay mystery novel "Stretched Love" through Tofu Ink Arts Press. Hi One Act Play "Reflections" has been chosen to be presented at the Region 8 KCACTF festival-Las Vegas, Nevada. Ten of his autobiographical stories are available on the Queer Slam Episode 21, podcast called "Just Gordon." Gordon has been a member of the oldest LGBTQ synagogue in the world Beth Chayim Chadishim since 1990.

Allie Cabal has been able to contribute their take on themes regarding identity and repression inspired by her peripatetic lifestyle and experiences in the modeling world.

Carrie Cantalupo (pen name) writes poetry and flash fiction and has been published in Pike's Peak, Making Waves, You Might Need to Hear This, Poetry Project Matters and The Closed Eye Open, in the anthology Transformational: Stories of Northern Arts and Culture and Walloon Review. Carrie lives in Maple City, Michigan in the Bohemian Wood and loves to hike, travel and read.

James Cariddi is a school psychologist who lives with his wife, two cats, and two dogs in Middletown, CT, where he enjoys growing vegetables, especially winter squash. He studied under John Murillo and Matthew Rohrer as undergrad at NYU.

Lucie Chou is an ecopoet whose work has appeared in the Entropy magazine, the Black Earth Institute Blog, the Tiny Seed Journal website and Plant Your Words Anthology. Her debut collection, Convivial Communiverse, is out from Atmosphere Press.

Katie Cloutte fell into writing poetry when she was thirteen. She spent four years soaking up some much needed poetry wisdom at the University of Richmond before receiving her MFA from New England College. She is currently living in Oxford, UK.

Willy Conley is an award-winning writer and photographer whose nine books include Photographic Memories, Plays of Our Own, Listening Through the Bone, and The Deaf Heart. Early in his career he worked as a medical photographer at leading hospitals in the U.S. before earning certification as a Registered Biological Photographer. He is professor emeritus of Theatre and Dance at Gallaudet University, the world's only liberal arts university for deaf and hard-of-hearing students in Washington, D.C.

Robert Esposito is an emerging contemporary artist whose work focuses on exploring the intersection between digital, spiritual, scientific, and abstract forms of art. His latest collection is entitled, "The New Point of View."

Peyton Fultz is a writer, editor, and painter from Poolesville, MD.

Addy Gravatte is a poet, artist, teacher and MFA student at CCA in San Francisco, California. They are especially in collage art and new forms of poetry.

Jessica de Koninck from Montclair, NJ, is the author of Cutting Room (Terrapin Books), and Repairs (Finishing Line Press). A 2023 winner of the DiBiase Poetry Contest. Her poems appear on the Writer's Almanac and Verse Daily.

Nooshin Hakim works at the intersection of sculpture, installation, and performance. Her practice investigates the material culture of conflict in a range of ways Javadi has received several awards and fellowships including Jerome Fellowship.

Christopher Hamel from Nebraska, earned an M.F.A. from Creighton University and has spent the entirety of his adult years teaching creative writing and playing in punk bands with varying degrees of success but with uninterrupted satisfaction.

Jennifer Handy is the author of the poetry chapbook *California Burning.* (Bottlecap Press, 2024) and *Dirt* (Finishing Line Press, 2025)

Natanjah Driscoll Harvey is a non-binary, Black, biracial poet, who lives half the year in Philadelphia, PA with their two orange cats.

Sam Heydt has established a significant international presence, having lived and worked in Paris, Venice, Amsterdam, Athens, Buenos Aires, Sydney, Reykjavík, Udaipur, and Vienna. Her academic career traversed Parsons School of Design, Cooper Union, Universiteit van Amsterdam, Universidad of Buenos Aires and La Sorbonne; further developing her practice through selective residencies across Iceland, Australia, New Zealand. HEYDT is the

founder and director of the esteemed creative agency, Jane Street
Studio, L.L.C.[est. 2012], as well as the visionary behind the gallery
and concept store KITSCH [est. 2020]. As a published author,
producer, and lifelong social activist and environmentalist, HEYDT
anchors her art in advocacy. Operating across a myriad of mediums,
she employs a range of recycled materials in her work, often
reinventing and trespassing their associative use. By juxtaposing
images of destruction with representations of the American Dream,
she confronts the disillusionment of our time with the ecological and
existential nightmare it is responsible for. HEYDT's work has graced
galleries, museums, art fairs, and film festivals worldwide, and sits in
eminent collections such as the Smithsonian and State Hermitage.

Aaron Hoge is a visual artist and a writer. With over 40 years of art-
making and multiple performances and exhibitions, Aaron is a
seasoned professional artist. Using the mediums of drawing, painting,
performance, video, writing, and photography Aaron's work explores
intersections between loneliness, becoming, homosocial relationships,
and futurity. Drawing inspiration from a wide range of sources such
as cave paintings, graffiti, Expressionism, Imagism, Vorticism,
English Literature, Western Esotericism, and Philosophy, his studio
practice represents an abiding interest in language, text, choreography,
semantics, poetry, and the creation of striking visual images. Aaron
becomes what he is through his visual art and writing. His lifework is
the integration of all aspects of the human personality.

Sara E. Hughes (aka sara e. hughes) is a Massachusetts-born poet, based in Ann Arbor, Michigan. She received an honorable mention for the American Poets College & University Prize in 2022. sara is the recipient of the 2021 Elaine V. Beilin, Howard Hirt, and Marjorie Sparrow Awards of Framingham State University. She holds a BA in English from Framingham State University and is a Nancy Craig Blackburn Fellow at Randolph College (MFA), Class of 2026. sara's work has appeared in *Obsidian: Literature & Arts in the African Diaspora, Superstition Review,* and *December Magazine.* Her work is forthcoming in *Poetry Magazine.*

Evan Huey is a queer, neurodivergent, local Canadian artist. They were born in Belleville, and grew up moving around between Canada and the US. Their artistic inspiration is drawn from independent artists and rotoscope animation. They hope to walk alongside people on their journey of self love by drawing them as they are, while turning their image into art. When Evan isn't drawing, they enjoy spending time with their cat, playing video games with friends, scrapbooking their adventures, and exploring local trails.

Jones Irwin teaches Philosophy and Education in Dublin, Republic of Ireland. His vision is of a postmodern existentialist, with a dash of noir mixed in with a progressivist ethic. He has been featured before in Tofu Ink.

Brian L. Jacobs is a poet and editor of Tofu Ink Arts Press along with Joseph Lee. Brian grew up in Southern California and has been teaching GATE English and Humanities for thirty-five years in both K-12 and college settings. He is 56 now and lives in Ann Arbor, Michigan and has been married for 20 years to Thye, a Professor of Nursing and a Nurse Practitioner. Brian was the assistant to the Poet's Allen Ginsberg and Julie Patton, during his time at Naropa in the mid 90's. During that time he walked half way around the world while on a peace pilgrimage with Buddhist monks commemorating WWII visiting Europe, the Middle East and India. Brian is also a three time Fulbright Scholar, which has allowed him to study in Brazil, where he studied its water issues; China, where he studied its vast 10,000 year history; and Japan, spending time to participate in a case study in one of its small towns near the Japanese Alps. He had also earned a National Endowment of Humanities grant to China, studying its philosophies and histories while living in Xi'an. He subsequently participated in a grant from Fund For Teachers visiting South Africa, Swaziland and Lesotho, plus earning other various grants that have taken him to places all over in the United States. He also taught teachers at a university in Fuzhou, China for five summers under grants from SABEH. Subsequently he has earned an Earthwatch grant to the rainforest of Ecuador, to study climate change and caterpillars and he recently earned another Earthwatch Senior Fellow Grant teaching teachers in Acadia, Maine studying climate change and crabs. Brian has been to over 100 countries and had visited all 50 states, practices Yoga and is a proud vegan. Brian's poetry has been published in several publications including, *Shiela-Na-Gig, the Crank, The South Florida Florida Poetry Journal, Progenitor Art and Literary Journal, GRIFFEL, Foxtail, Rip Rap, The Bangalore Review, Sunspot Lit, Anthropod, Pa'Lante, Dark Moon Lilith Press, Black Tape Press, Genre, Inky Blue/Celery, Red Dancefloor Press, Entelechy, 1844 Pine Street, Pasta Poetics, Trouble, In Parenthesis, Unbound Anthology, Landlocked and Praxis.* Brian recently had published an epic novel, HOMOCAUST.

B. A. Kocsis is an Australian collage artist and poet whose work has been published in Into The Void Magazine. Kocsis served in the Royal Australian Infantry. He holds a BA from the University of Queensland and is undertaking a Masters of Teaching.

Karin Falcone Krieger has her recent writing and art published in The Decadent Review, Hunger Mountain, Grande Dame, Viewless Wings, Tupelo Quarterly, and in the anthology, A physical book which compiles conceptual books (Partial Press, 2022). She taught writing as an adjunct instructor for 20 years, and was an adjunct union representative.

She earned an MFA is from The Jack Kerouac School of Disembodied Poetics at Naropa, and published the zine artICHOKE from 1989-2008. She occasionally types poems in public space on a 100 year old typewriter.

Mario Loprete, an Italian artist working at the intersection of painting and sculpture, transforms raw urban materials like cement and plaster into powerful reflections on memory, identity, and modern life. His use of concrete, a material rooted in both ancient Rome and contemporary architecture, symbolizes permanence and collective history, while fragile plaster suggests the vulnerability of human experience. Merging these elements, Loprete creates textured, relic-like works that capture the tension between the fleeting and the eternal. Often incorporating graffiti and portraits of hip-hop artists, his art immortalizes voices of urban culture, grounding them in materials that echo the streets they emerged from. Through this fusion of material and meaning, Loprete's work becomes a poetic archive of our time, preserving what is usually lost and giving form to what cities remember.

Cameron Charles Martin comes from California but does not currently make a home in a specific place. His writing has not previously appeared in publication. He likes perfumes that are a little stinky.

JP McGowan is a young writer and poet from Richmond, Virginia. He leads a noisy life in the city with no spouse or pets.

Grant McGrath is a Brooklyn based abstract painter.

Marl Meier His formal art education began with a photography class at The New Orleans Academy of Fine Arts. He has worked primarily in linocut, watercolor, and ink since then. A member of the Authors Guild, his writing has appeared in various publications and on stage.

River Morel is a SUNY Purchase student of psychology and photography, with plans to later pursue an MFA in poetry. He is French-German-American, raised in Brooklyn, NY. River is the winner of a Silver Key National Scholastic Writing Award.

Andrew Lincoln Nelson is an artist in Arizona. He produces detailed graphite drawings of futuristic arid landscapes containing machine-creatures, alien plants and other strange conglomerations. He studied art at the University of Wyoming and also engineering at NCSU. He has worked as a researcher in robotics, cell and molecular biology and in the design of electric machines. Some of his work depicts ideas from speculative biology and non-earthly forms of evolution. Nelson uses only traditional hand-drawing methods with the majority of his work being graphite pencil on heavy drawing board.

Adele Nwankwo is a genderfluid member of the Nigerian diaspora. They are a healthcare worker by trade, but have recently taken up writing. Their poetry is inspired and encouraged by figures like Gwendolyn Brooks and Douglas Kearney.

Mary-Jo Okawa MJ is a silk painter whose radiant, joy-filled creations are a vibrant fusion of East and West. Based in Chandler, Arizona, MJ draws from her Japanese family ties and the natural beauty of the Southwest to create artwork that feels both timeless and alive. Her work bridges traditional Japanese silk painting techniques with a bold, contemporary aesthetic—metallic gutta outlines, luminous jewel tones, and mesmerizing textures created with salt, sugar, and alcohol bring each piece to life with energy and emotion. Originally from Mountain View, California, MJ's love for color, movement, and nature runs deep. After decades as a celebrated arts educator and founder of Copperstar Repertory Company—a cherished Arizona theatre company that welcomed artists of all ages and abilities—MJ has returned to her visual art practice with joyful abandon. Copperstar produced 43 inclusive productions and hosted thriving summer camps for hundreds of children annually, leaving a lasting creative imprint on the community. MJ's art celebrates nature's magic—landscapes, botanicals, and shimmering skies that uplift the spirit. Her silk paintings are immersive and emotionally resonant, offering viewers a moment of serenity and awe. Whether glowing with a quiet stillness or bursting with saturated color, her works are known for sparking wonder and connection. Her paintings have been exhibited in galleries, shows and fine art festivals across Arizona, California, New Mexico, Colorado, New York, and Missouri. A proud mother of two multi-talented adult children, MJ is passionate about inspiring joy, reflection, and meaningful conversations through her work. She continues to explore new themes and techniques while remaining rooted in her mission: to create beauty that heals, uplifts, and connects us all.

Nik Orlando form Los Angeles, has been focused on resin sculptures and paintings for the past several years. Most recently he converted his garage into the Star Love Monkey Studio. He is also interested in textiles and fashion design. Currently, sculpture and fashion seem to be the perfect combination for Nik's passion for experimentation and backwards planning; thinking with the end in mind. Nik is obsessed with the concepts of layers, reflections, patterns and symbols. He is driven by the unexpected combination of any of these concepts in the hopes to elicit memories of the past and joy in the future. These past few years, inspiration has come from music, wallpaper, reflection, birds, casinos and komorebi (木漏れ日), the Japanese word for "light through trees" which describes the dappled, dancing patterns of sunlight that filter through the leaves of trees. Nik believes everyday is a day to live your look and be unexpectedly inspired by what you see and hear.

Debbra Palmer is a poet and visual artist living in Idaho's Treasure Valley with her wife. She received her MFA at Pacific University, and publishes literary-themed cartoons in Northwest Review where she is an assistant poetry editor.

Claudio Parentela (is a prolific and eclectic Italian artist whose work spans illustration, painting, digital art, collage, photography, comics, mail art, textile art, and experimental publishing. Active internationally since the 1990s, his wildly distinctive, surreal, and anarchic style has been featured in hundreds of underground and contemporary art zines, journals, and exhibitions across Europe, the U.S., South America, and Asia. He has collaborated with numerous artists, poets, musicians (especially in the industrial, noise, and experimental scenes), and independent publishers, contributing artwork, comics, and tarot decks. His art has been exhibited in spaces from Milan to New York, Berlin to Tel Aviv, and has appeared in festivals such as BREAK 21 in Slovenia. He remains a constant presence in the global alternative art scene through countless exhibitions, mail art projects, and multimedia collaborations.

Xiaoqiu Qiu is a poet, novelist and translator from Shanghai. His poetry has been published in Meridian, Reed Magazine, Broad River Review and more. Currently, he is a Black Mountain Institute Fellow and a PhD student of Creative Writing at UNLV.

Octavio Quintanilla is the author of the poetry collection, *If I Go Missing*, the founder and director of the literature & arts festival, VersoFrontera, publisher of Alabrava Press, and former Poet Laureate of San Antonio, TX. He teaches Literature and Creative Writing at Our Lady of the Lake University.

Raymond Rosales is a Bay Area artist. He has pieces up in the Art Thou Gallery as well as their sister gallery NYC&T.

Ken Edward Rutkowski is an artist/ writer living in southern Vietnam. While in Asia, he has traveled around Vietnam, Cambodia, Malaysia, the Philippines, Taiwan, Indonesia, Thailand, Hong Kong, Borneo and Sri Lanka. His work has appeared in Mad Swirl, Tofu Ink Arts Press, Scapegoat Review, Unlikely Stories, The New Post-literate, High Shelf Press, The Beatnik Cowboy, Fiction International, Synchronized Chaos, The Fiction Pool, Paragraph Line, The Journal of Experimental Fiction, Fiction Daily and Borders: An Anthology of Whatcom County Writers. He has received an Honorable Mention for the Tofu Ink Arts Press Poetry Prize in Honor of Reza Abdoh (2021) and included in the Best of Mad Swirl 2022 Anthology.

Aleksandra Scepanovic is a New York sculptor whose work explores the human condition through fragmented forms, celebrating wholeness amidst fracture and transformation. Her sculptural language, rooted in clay, metal, plaster, stone, and found materials, draws from her own experience of migratory displacement and her ongoing quest for a true likeness of identity suspended between war,

peace, and culture. Before devoting herself to sculpture, she was a war
reporter in the Balkans, a journey that profoundly informed her
exploration of endurance and the fragile boundaries between form
and expectation. In addition to her sculptural practice, she curates
site-responsive exhibitions that transform overlooked spaces into
temporary cultural venues, fostering dialogue between artists and
communities. She currently works between Woodstock and New
York City, where she is represented by Amos Eno Gallery.

Samantha R. Sharp is a neurodivergent writer and PhD candidate in
Comparative Literature at SUNY Binghamton, where she studies
ecopoetics and political ecology. She is Poetry Editor for Midway
Journal, and has work in Cleaver, Dipity, and others.

Melinda R. Smith is an artist and writer whose work explores the
liminal regions between reality and fantasy, using tropes strongly
reminiscent of childhood play. With her lifelong love of storytelling,
she conceives of her pictures as staged theatrical scenes that tell
archetypal stories whose roots reach for the dark core of memory and
truth. In 2022, following the upheavals of Covid, she left Los
Angeles, California, after 30 years to return to her hometown of
Kalamazoo, Michigan.

Michael O. Starr has been writing poetry since 2003. He has experience
editorially as well as creatively, being published in smaller offbeat journals like
Lipstick Party and Aberration Labyrinth. He has been published multiple times
in BlazeVOX. Still awaiting a contract for full- length titles, he has a backload of
approximately 8 years of written and unedited work looking to see the light. For
now, he lives in his cave. Former biologist & competitive tennis player currently
aimimg for a career in web development. Co-founder and editor of [Alternate
Route].Stylistically transgressive and daring, often dejected from being alive by
close circles in the State.

George L Stein is a photographer from the greater NYC area
working in the street and surreal genres. George has had success in
publishing photos in lit magazines as well as exhibits at LACP and
Praxis Gallery.

Shelley Stoehr teaches writing at Southern Connecticut State
University and is the winner of a 2023 de Groot Foundation Writer of
Note grant. Shelley has received awards from *The North American
Review, New Millenium Sunshots, Writer's Digest,* WOW: Women on
Writing, and the ALA. Her poetry chapbook, *Glitterotica,* was
published in 2023 by Dancing Girl Press.

Morgan Stone earned an MA from NYU in counseling, a BA from
Tulane University in psychology, and is a certified trauma coach.
After spending her days working as a school counselor and caring for
her three children, she spends her nights writing.

Ali Telmesani is a Creative Writing PhD Candidate at Swansea
University in South Wales, UK. His 2018 publication by Claritas
Books, London, is entitled 'House of Abbas: The Legacy of Harun al-
Rashid'. Whilst pillaging chariot battles from the Iliad and Aeneid for
ideas, Ali developed a burning desire to hear dactylic or 'heroic'
hexameter in the original Homeric Greek and Latin, but knew neither.
Down and out, he resolved to compose his own hexametic poem in
English instead, then deflect blame by placing it in the mouth of a
principle character/narrator/perfect fall girl, Aya of Herak, from his
doctoral project tentatively entitled 'The Zagra Valley Codices'

Sona Verdi writes stories and develops 35mm film from her New
York City apartment.

Joelle Wilcock is a nature photographer/digital artist ready to share her art with the world. Her passion for creating digital media full of passion and human emotions is growing everyday. Every piece of photography/digital art she creates represents the emotions she experiences as a mum raising a special needs child. It is her mission to help educate people about the invisible disability, Autism.

Rex Wilder is a mixed pictorial artist and poet living in Venice, California. He has several recent magazine covers and portfolios to his credit and 4 books of poetry. This work is from his upcoming gallery show, Phases of Honeymoon.

Eric Wittkopf (he/him) holds a couple degrees and has published a couple poems. He has works forthcoming in places like Wild Roof Journal, Half and One, and JanusWords. He is a Pushcart nominee, and won first place in a themed contest run by House Journal in 2021.